THE COMPLETE BOOK OF
HORSE AND PONY CARE

THE COMPLETE BOOK OF
HORSE AND PONY CARE

MICHAEL JANSON

AND

JULIANA KEMBALL-WILLIAMS

SMITHMARK

For Hannah and our first pony, Tom

PICTURE CREDITS

Bruce Coleman 65 (all), 66; /Eric Crichton 52 (bottom left); /Christer Fredriksson 8, 72; / M. Timothy O'Keefe 70; /Fritz Frenzel 17 (bottom); /Hans Reinhard 6, 56, 88; /Kim Taylor 2; **Bob Langrish** 16, 25, 29, 31, 32, 33, 34, 35, 37, 38, 40, 41, 43, 44, 47 (left), 48 (right), 50, 51, 52 (top right and bottom right), 53, 54, 58, 60, 61, 62 (all), 63, 74 (top and bottom), 75, 76 (all), 77 (top), 81 (bottom), 85, 86 (bottom), 90, 91 (bottom); **Only Horses** 11, 12, 13, 14 (left and right), 17 (top), 18, 19, 20, 21, 23 (all), 24, 26, 27 (top and bottom), 28, 39, 42, 45, 46, 47 (right), 48 (left), 49, 59, 67 (top and bottom), 6, 8, 69, 71, 77 (bottom), 78, 80, 81 (top), 84, 86 (top), 87, 91 (top)

Every effort has been made to trace the copyright holders and we apologize in advance for any unintentional omissions. We would be pleased to insert the appropriate acknowledgement in any subsequent edition of this publication.

This edition published in the USA in 1996 by SMITHMARK Publishers,
a division of U.S. Media Holdings, Inc.,
16 East 32nd Street, New York, NY 10016

First published in Great Britain in 1996 by Parragon Book Service Ltd

SMITHMARK books are available for bulk purchase for sales promotion and premium use. For details write or call the manager of special sales, SMITHMARK Publishers, 16 east 32nd Street, New York, NY 10016; (212) 532-6600.

ISBN: [TO COME]
10 9 8 7 6 5 4 3 2 1

Produced by Haldane Mason, London

Editor: Charles Dixon-Spain
Designer: Zoë Mellors
Illustrations: Rob McFarlane

Printed in Italy

CONTENTS

9   CHAPTER 1

Owning and Buying your own Horse

CHAPTER 2   29

The Care and Maintenance of Tack

43   CHAPTER 3

Caring for your Horse

CHAPTER 4   57

Training

79   CHAPTER 5

Showing and Competing

CHAPTER 6   89

Your Horse's Health

96   *Index*

INTRODUCTION

Horses and humans have lived and worked together for more than 5,000 years,

with the horse providing transport, being the prime draught animal, warhorse and sporting

companion. Today, after losing the competition with motor transport, the horse

is mostly used for sport and recreation.

More people are riding now than ever before – the horse has retained its magic and its dignity in the fast track of modern living and is as popular as ever. Horses are versatile creatures and have something to offer to everybody from racing to showing, leisure riding to eventing, show-jumping to playing polo.

What you choose to do is your individual choice, but how you choose what to do is the same – the relationship between the horse and rider is the most important thing. Experience breeds confidence in both horse and rider and that only comes with spending time together.

In this book we have laid out the basic needs of the horse and rider, from choosing the correct mount to learning to ride, from caring for your horse's needs to ensuring its health. We have honestly offered advice that has been gathered over many years, but no two horses are alike and only you can gather the practical experience, make the correct decisions and learn from your own mistakes.

For some people, horses become a time-consuming passion for life, some may say an obsession, but if any animal deserves it, it is the horse. If you can find that perfect partnership then your life will be richer.

Happy riding!

Chapter 1
OWNING AND BUYING YOUR OWN HORSE

Learning to ride is the beginning of what can be a lifetime's pleasure

of owning and caring for your horse or pony. From the beginning,

however, it is essential to learn properly and to understand the

responsibility of ownership.

LEARNING TO RIDE

There is no age limit to riding. Indeed, a horse gives both young and old legs a greater opportunity for mobility, and toddlers and senior citizens can enjoy riding as much as anybody else. Most people's first experience of horse-riding is being led on a pony or donkey along the beach or at some kind of fair. This is often enough to enthuse the youngster to learn to ride properly – and if they want to learn, they should be taught properly by a qualified instructor from the start at an approved and recognized riding stable. Bad habits learned early are difficult to unlearn later.

The qualified instructor also has the experience of the differing abilities of beginners and can match a horse and pony in their stable to the abilities and temperament of the novice. Usually lessons are hourly and the rate will vary from stable to stable and will cover a period of weeks on a regular basis. Weekends are the most usual, although in summer with longer days, afternoon and evening lessons can be arranged. A top-class riding establishment may well have an indoor menage, or a flood-lit outdoor menage, and will be less dependent on the vagaries of climate and weather.

LEFT: *Swedish full-blood and foal grazing in summer.*

All equipment is supplied – horse, tack and riding hat – and all you need to do is wear the appropriate clothing and turn up on time and regularly. Long gaps between rides can result in a lack of confidence and time wasted re-learning things you have forgotten. Generally, you will be taught in a class of varying numbers of people.

A good course of instruction will not only teach you the basics of riding, but also how to look after a horse properly, including grooming and stable routine. After learning your skills in the riding school you will then be in a position to decide how you want to develop your riding enjoyment. There are two main routes to take, neither of which excludes the other. Simply riding out in the country, with no competitive intentions, is all that many people want. The thrill of riding in open country and having access to places difficult to reach on foot, or not at all by motor transport, coupled with a horseback-eye's view of the wildlife is an experience hard to match.

The other route is to enter regularly organized competitive events such as showing, show-jumping or eventing, where both horse and rider can display and improve their skills alongside other interested horse owners.

BUYING A HORSE OR PONY

Once you have become certain that horse-riding is the sport or hobby that you wish to pursue, then you will probably consider buying your own horse or pony. There are several advantages to owning your own and several disadvantages – all of which should be weighed carefully before you make your decision. The purchase of a horse or pony is a serious commitment which can give years of pleasure or could be a very disappointing experience.

THE BONUSES

Owning your own horse allows you to ride whenever you want, rather than having to book designated hours at a riding stable. But more importantly it allows you to develop a riding relationship with one horse so that together you can learn and improve. Horse and rider will begin to understand one another's temperament and moods, and if the rider is consistent with his or her signals the horse will learn how to respond. A horse that is ridden by several different people each week, and in all probability they will be of differing height, weight and riding ability, cannot be expected to be consistent in the performance it gives. And having your own horse, like any other animal, teaches you the need for responsibility and compassion.

THINGS TO CONSIDER

Horses take time, money and an investment in care that far exceeds that necessary for any other pet such as a cat or a dog. It is essential to be honest as to how much time you can commit and how much you can afford, because the horse will need both in varying amounts, depending on the breed of horse, how it is kept and for what purpose it is used.

The purchase price of a horse is only the beginning. Tack is a major cost item, although many horses are sold with their tack included in the selling price, or as an option at a discounted price. The monthly costs of feeding, and general up-keep can quickly exceed the original purchase price of many horses. Grooming equipment, cleaning materials and sundries necessary for good daily care are minor costs but can add up over time. While the costs of keeping a horse can vary quite considerably, you will need to have a realistic idea of the overall expenses.

One of the most important decisions to be made is where to keep your horse. Unless you are lucky enough to own your own land or have space for stabling, you will have to pay to keep your horse. The cheapest option is to pay field rent, where you hire a pasture or paddock – usually shared with other owners – and undertake the feeding and caring for the horse yourself. Some

FINANCIAL CHECKLIST

The cost of a horse has many components beyond the initial purchase price. Some can be planned for and some not, and there are many 'hidden extras'. The following is a general guide to the range of costs one might plan for with notations of some of the additions you may find essential. Draw up a full list with real and estimated monthly or weekly costs before you decide to purchase.

BASIC SUBSISTENCE: livery, field rent, feed and bedding

TACK:

BASICS: saddle, bridle, headcollar, lead rope, tack rack

ADDITIONAL: martingale, special bits, lunging rope

HORSE CLOTHING/PROTECTIVE EQUIPMENT: winter rug, sweat rug, bandages, working boots

GROOMING EQUIPMENT: curry comb, brushes, hoof pick

CLEANING EQUIPMENT: saddle soap, sponges

HEALTH PRODUCTS: linament, sprays, hoof oil, etc.

FOR THE RIDER:

EVERYDAY: hat, trousers, boots

SHOWING/HUNTING/EVENTING: jacket, boots, shirt, ties, stock and stock-pins, gloves, back-protector

SHOWING COSTS:

TRANSPORT

TRAVEL PROTECTION

ENTRY FEES AND SUBSISTENCE (e.g. cost of handlers, overnight stabling)

SPECIAL TACK/CLOTHING

VETERINARY CHARGES:

REGULAR ATTENDANCE (e.g. worming, injections)

ATTENDANCE TO INJURIES/SUDDEN PROBLEMS

FARRIER COSTS

INSURANCE

ABOVE: *Hardy native breeds are tolerant of most conditions.*

breeds of horses are happy to be kept out in a field all year round, in fact some prefer this to being stabled, while others will need permanent shelter. Different breeds and individual horses have different requirements.

At the other end of the spectrum you can pay for full livery at a stable and they will undertake to look after the horse for you throughout the year. While this is more expensive, it can give you access to many shared facilities which you might not be able to provide yourself, such as indoor riding facilities, a range of practice jumps, shared transport and handling costs to shows. For the beginner, the camaraderie, shared interests and learning about horses, which can be gained from being part of a group or stable, is a wonderful experience.

A compromise on full livery is that some stables offer part-livery whereby the stable takes on the care but will use the horse to hire out to other clients. This has the advantage of reducing costs but may reduce your available riding time and you have no guarantee about the ability of the other riders. Find out at your local stables what is available and the exact costs before you even think of buying.

Another popular option is to share a horse. This is often most suitable for two children with a first pony and has the advantage of testing the actual time and commitment that can be given. Care and costs are reduced and the only real problem is ensuring that everyone does their fair share of the work and enjoys a fair share of the riding.

There are also a wide range of other regular costs to be taken into account – insurance, veterinarian's fees, regular shoeing and replacement and repair of tack when needed. If you want to show your horse then there will be additional travel expenses, entry fees and extra grooming equipment, not to mention appropriate clothing for the rider. Add these to your livery costs to get the a fairly accurate idea of the monthly outgoings.

All this is not designed to discourage you from buying a horse, but to make sure you understand the kind of commitment you will have to make. Owning a horse also involves the rest of the family's time, as so many parents will know from having to plan their vacations around the needs of the horse or the timing of a show, so make sure you warn them that their time might be needed too.

WHERE TO BUY

There are several avenues open to those wishing to buy a horse or pony. If you are already taking lessons, or regularly riding at a reputable riding school or stables, the owners will usually be willing to help you find the right animal to suit your ability and pocket, especially if you intend to keep the horse at livery with them. At local shows and Pony Club events you may get to hear about horses or ponies that are for sale and if you can see them in action it gives you the chance to assess their abilities and also the ability of the rider in handling it. Horse magazines and many local newspapers, especially in rural areas, carry advertisements in their 'For Sale' columns. Another possibility is to buy at one of the many regular horse-sales that are held around the country. Although auctions can provide a bargain, they can also present you with expensive trouble if you are not expert in choosing horses. Remember you will not always be able to try out a horse beforehand. The golden rule is: if you do not know exactly what you are looking for, always seek independent expert advice.

THE HORSE FOR YOU

When choosing a horse there are certain questions that you have to ask yourself and answer honestly. These apply especially to children who may not be experienced riders and yet want their first pony.

First, how accomplished are you as a rider? A weekly ride on a riding school pony which has been schooled to be fairly docile and worked hard does not necessarily qualify you for a horse that has been ridden and jumped hard. If you are not strong or experienced enough to control it from the beginning you will end up with a badly behaved horse, possibly forever, and potentially broken bones for yourself. Do not think you can grow into a horse or pony. A pony that is too headstrong for a child can very quickly ruin their dream of riding.

Second, for what purpose do you intend to use your horse? Do you want to show-jump or event, or do you just want a handy family horse that you can hack out with? The answer will immediately rule out certain types and breeds of horse, but there is still a wide range of choice.

Size, age, sex and breed are all factors which you will need to consider. While much of this is a matter of personal preference, there are a few general guidelines. Young horses of 5-6 years lack experience and are best avoided by less experienced riders. The older a horse, the more sensible and well-schooled it tends to be, although it has also had a greater opportunity to acquire bad habits which may be difficult to correct. Among riding horses the choice is typically between mares and geldings. Opinion differs on the merits of each, but because mares are subject to the regular breeding cycle, a gelding might be preferable.

The choice of a horse versus a pony is largely an issue of size, balance and control. The physical size of a rider relative to his or her mount will affect the balance and comfort of both horse and rider, as well as being visually important. Remember, too, that riders grow but horses and ponies do not.

In choosing your horse you may wish to select a particular breed either for its appearance or for the type of riding you are planning. Different breeds have different physical characteristics of size and colour, and also vary in temperament and in the level of care they require. Cross-bred native breeds are usually the best option for a first purchase as their temperament is more gentle and if you only have a field and shelter in which to keep your pony, it will happily survive in its rugged native conditions.

MAKING YOUR CHOICE

Once you have found a potentially suitable horse it is time to take a closer look at it. Take an experienced person with you because no amount of reading will substitute for practical experience. Equally important, go with an open mind and be prepared to refuse. It is easy to become carried away with the excitement of having your own horse or pony, and want to buy the first one you see. The more animals you see, the better the chance of making the right match, and the more you will learn.

When assessing a horse you are checking for three things – its temperament and social manners, its overall health and fitness and what is known as its conformation. Basically, conformation is the term for a horse's physical characteristics and the proportions of

ABOVE: *A good-tempered horse is essential for young riders.*

its body, legs, neck and head in relationship to each other. Obviously this will vary between different breeds, but there are a few basics which can affect the way a horse moves and performs, as well as its overall attractiveness.

THE HORSE'S CHARACTER

Perhaps the most important point to remember when choosing is that horses are like people, they have their own personalities and habits, and you need to get to know as much as you can about their character before making your decision.

Horses can vary greatly in temperament: some are kind and calm, others are moody and badly behaved; some have been brought up with good manners while others have not; and some stabled horses develop vices which are incurable – these are known as cribbing and weaving. Cribbing involves the continual biting of the stable door and walls, while weaving is rocking from front foot to front foot. If either of these traits are exhibited then the horse is best avoided. Look out for how relaxed the horse is – does he stay calm when you enter the stable or does he shy away? Does he try to get out as soon as you open the door?

If your potential purchase is turned out in a field, watch to see how he gets on with the other animals. Does he run, shy or bite

ABOVE: *Shetland ponies are popular with very small children, but can be very badly behaved.*

when other horses come near? Does he respond to the owner's arrival or is there a chase round the field to capture him before he can be tacked up? Watch carefully how he responds when being bridled and saddled. Does he stand still or continually try to move away? How easy is it to get his head down and will he take the bit easily? Does he stand still and quiet when being groomed? Check how easily he lifts his feet to have his hooves picked. See how he responds to verbal commands. The more co-operative the horse, the better it will be for you.

One important point which is often overlooked is how easy a horse is to box. A horse which is difficult to box can take up a huge amount of time when trying to transport him, as well as being very frustrating and potentially dangerous for both the horse and its handlers.

HEALTH AND FITNESS

An untrained eye can easily overlook problems, and if you are seriously interested in a particular horse or pony, it is always best to have it checked by a veterinarian. No horse is perfect, and a vet's advice can help you distinguish between major and minor problems. Some horses may appear sound but gradually develop problems over time because of subtle defects or past injuries. Professional advice can help identify these kind of potential troublespots.

There are a number of things which you can do when viewing any horse for the first time which give a general indication of its overall health. Begin with the head: the eyes should be clear and bright, not sticky or watery; the nostrils should be free of any heavy mucous and quite clear. Check around the mouth, particularly at the corners, for any cuts or bleeding – this usually indicates that heavy force has been used on the bit by either an inexperienced rider or because the horse is difficult to control. Also, be sure to watch out for any sign of persistent coughing.

The legs and feet are the most crucial part of a sound horse, and it is here that most major problems occur. Look closely for any scarring which indicates a previous injury, or any signs of swelling, particularly around the knees and hocks. It is also a good

ABOVE: *Before you purchase a horse, a full veterinary inspection is essential.*

LEFT: *The distinctively shaped head of the Arab horse.*

idea to run your hand down the horse's legs, feeling for bumps or swelling that may not be obvious to the eye and to check for any areas which are particularly hot, indicating inflammation and possibly injury.

Check the horse's feet closely on the outside for any cracks or deep ridges that may indicate a previous problem. The hooves should be quite cool to the touch. Check the underside of the foot. The horn or sole of the foot should be hard, smooth and dipped in slightly – do not consider a horse with a spongy horn. The frog, which is a 'V'-shaped area running from the horse's heel, should be free from any major cracks and quite pliable.

Finally, run your hands over the entire horse's body: this allows you to check for any lumps, sores or areas where the horse may be sensitive. Inspect the condition of the coat which should be glossy and free of any scales or heavy dandruff. Look out for bald patches or signs of rubbing, particularly at the top of the tail, which may suggest an irritation or could also result from bad stable habits.

CONFORMATION POINTS

A horse's body structure, or conformation, can tell you about potential health and fitness problems, but is equally important in determining a horse's quality and physical attractiveness. For each breed there is a different ideal configuration of, for example, the shape and length of the neck. However, there are a few general features which go to make up a good-looking and well-structured animal whatever its breed. The most important thing to assess is the condition of the legs and feet, as the way they are set and the way a horse stands will decide if the horse will give you a good,

smooth ride or be prone to injury. First, look at the horse side on; ideally, the foreleg hoof should be positioned below a point midway between the shoulder and the elbow, and the hindleg hoof should sit at a midway point between the buttock and stifle point. The pastern connecting the horse's hoof and fetlock should angle forward so that the fetlock is on a line well behind the toe. Any variations on this and the horse could well be prone to lameness and tendon strains.

Second, view the horse from the back to check its stance. The legs should be straight and point directly forward. If the hocks turn in on each other and are close together, then the horse is cow-hocked, and the bones and tendons will be under strain. If the hocks turn out, the horse looks bow-legged, and this will be even more wearing on the legs.

More generally, there are a number of good points to look for. The head should be well-proportioned in relation to the body, the eyes large and set well apart and the ears not too large and set towards the front of the head. The shape of the nose will vary with the breed. Arabians tend to have dish-shaped faces while heavy horses often have noses which curve downwards. As a general rule, the shape of a horse's head when seen in profile should be quite straight with a gently sloping muzzle.

Other good points are a deep broad chest, sloping shoulders and well-rounded hindquarters which give an indication of the horse's power. The neck is an important part of the horse's overall appearance. It should be curved and crested at the top, not U-shaped, and the back relatively straight with only a slight dip between the withers and top of the rump.

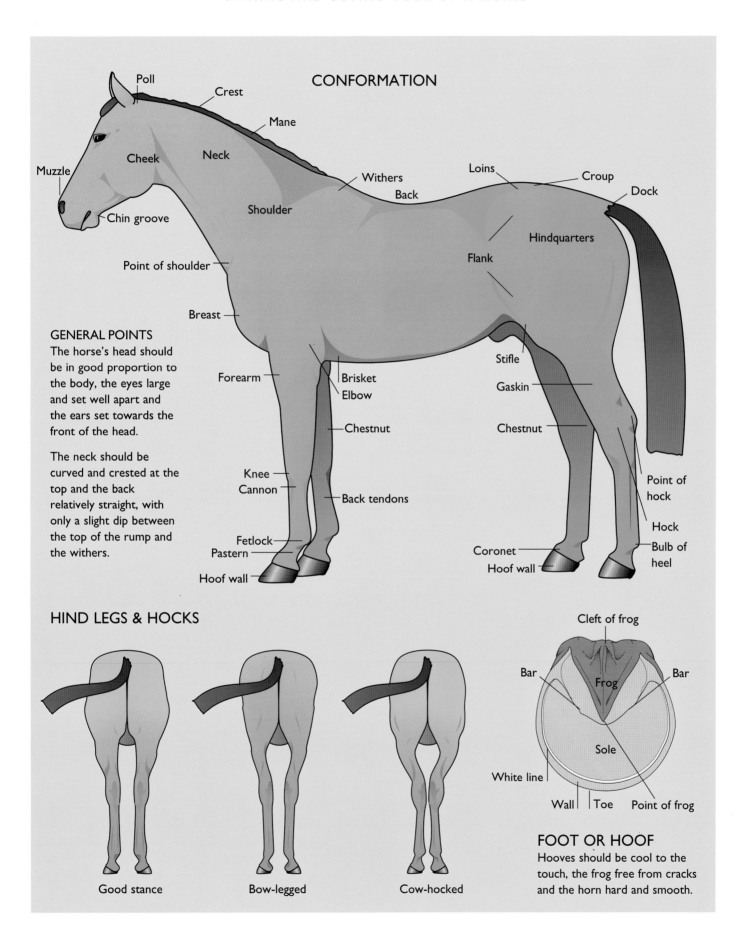

CONFORMATION

Poll
Crest
Mane
Cheek
Neck
Muzzle
Withers
Loins
Croup
Dock
Back
Chin groove
Shoulder
Hindquarters
Point of shoulder
Flank
Breast

GENERAL POINTS

The horse's head should be in good proportion to the body, the eyes large and set well apart and the ears set towards the front of the head.

The neck should be curved and crested at the top and the back relatively straight, with only a slight dip between the top of the rump and the withers.

Forearm
Brisket
Elbow
Stifle
Gaskin
Chestnut
Chestnut
Knee
Cannon
Back tendons
Point of hock
Fetlock
Pastern
Hock
Coronet
Bulb of heel
Hoof wall
Hoof wall

HIND LEGS & HOCKS

Good stance
Bow-legged
Cow-hocked

Cleft of frog
Bar
Frog
Bar
Sole
White line
Wall
Toe
Point of frog

FOOT OR HOOF

Hooves should be cool to the touch, the frog free from cracks and the horn hard and smooth.

15

Check how easy he is to mount and whether he stands still or needs to be held. Begin slowly by walking and turning so that you can get the feel of each other. Note how he responds to the bit and whether he walks on a loose rein or needs to be held back. Stop occasionally and see if he stands still and quietly. Try backing up a few steps, which is a good test of manners and responsiveness.

You may need to get used to the feel of an individual horse's gaits as these can vary quite a bit – what is a comfortable ride for one person may not be for another. At trot and canter check the horse's balance and whether he travels in a straight line with equal pressure on both reins, rather than pulling to one side. Work the horse in both clockwise and anti-clockwise directions to be sure it will take both leads at the canter, and is not unbalanced or stiff in one particular direction.

If you decide to try jumping, be aware that some horses have a tendency to rush into fences, pulling strongly and getting in under the obstacle before taking-off. This makes for an uncomfortable and sometimes dangerous ride as they are more likely to refuse or to 'cat-jump' the fence. Try a variety of different fences if possible, because sometimes normally willing jumpers refuse point-blank certain kinds of fences, and no amount of coaxing or force will persuade them.

Remember when testing a horse that some may behave differently in a familiar environment compared with relatively strange surroundings. Also, if trying out a horse in an indoor menage it is a good idea to test him in the open as well. Some horses are fine inside an enclosure, but become uncontrollable in open spaces.

Having experienced the horse in action you should be in a good position to judge its suitability for you. If you have encountered a number of problems remember that few horses have perfect manners and that many bad habits can be corrected with persistent schooling, but this can involve considerable time, expense and frustration if you choose to do it yourself. Schooling also requires a minimum level of ability and experience. If you are a beginner it is better to try and find an experienced horse who can teach you what good manners are.

In making your decision, weigh the pros and cons carefully and do not be pressurized if you have even one per cent of doubt.

THE HORSE IN ACTION

After this initial inspection it is time to see the horse in action. Ask the owner to lead him in hand, walking away from you and trotting back. The horse should move with a straight action and not throw out a leg or cross his forelegs. Ask the owner to ride him and put him through his paces – walking, trotting, cantering and maybe jumping – to see how he responds.

Next, ride him yourself. Before mounting you should ask the owner what cues the horse expects in order to get him to change gaits, as these may be different from those you have been taught.

You can always come back another time. This is an important decision for both horse and rider – you have to be sure that you can live happily together.

Most owners who are selling may be prepared to let you take a horse for a short trial period. During this time you should spend as much time with the horse as possible to make sure you really can get on. Perhaps the new, unfamiliar surroundings and new companions do not suit your new friend, or maybe you feel less at ease than you thought you would when you first saw one another. Ask a veterinarian to give you a written report confirming that the horse is healthy. Now, and only now, is the time to agree to purchase, and ensure that you receive the registration documents and current proof of innoculations when you complete the transaction.

ABOVE: *Andalusian horse.*
BELOW: *Arabian foal already showing its lively spirit.*

THE BREEDS

ABOVE: *An Arabian mare putting her foal through its paces.*

There are a vast number of different breeds throughout the world and native horses and ponies have been bred with imported bloodstock for hundreds of years. Breeds differ in size, temperament and looks, and it is perhaps difficult today to imagine the need to have so many different breeds when horses are now mostly used for leisure riding or racing. Not long ago however, when horses were still the prime form of transport and motive force on farms and in towns, they had to be bred for different purposes – speed, strength and stamina were all required to differing degrees depending on the job to be done.

Most horses of recognized breeds will be registered with an official breeder association. Without an official certificate showing the horse's pedigree it is difficult to establish the purity of any horse's breeding, so if this is important to you, make sure it can be corroborated.

ABOVE: *The Arabian is noted for strength and elegance.*

THE ARABIAN

The Arabian is the classic horse, selectively bred for generations in the Middle East for speed, strength, spirit, stamina and elegance in equal measure. Its dominant genes have been introduced into the blood-lines of nearly every kind of horse to strengthen and refine the breed. The Arabian is a spirited horse and needs a spirited and competent rider if it is to be ridden at its best and is not suitable for a novice. Size: Up to 15.2 h.h.

THE THOROUGHBRED

Thoroughbreds were bred as racehorses to be bigger, stronger and faster. Stallions of Arabian stock were imported into Europe to breed with native mares during the 17th and early 18th centuries, starting a breeding line which has been exported all over the world. Now, there are Thoroughbred horse studs on every continent. Thoroughbreds crossed with other native breeds have produced great show-jumpers, eventers and hunters. All Thoroughbreds are extremely fast, especially over short distances. Size: Up to 17 h.h.

The Welsh Mountain: An excellent and reliable children's pony, the Welsh Mountain is hardy, intelligent and good-looking, in part due to an early influx of Arab and Thoroughbred blood. Size: Up to 12 h.h.

The Welsh Pony: The traditional shepherd's pony, the Welsh Pony is sure-footed with a good temperament that makes it a good children's riding pony. Size: Up to 13.2 h.h.

The Welsh Pony – Cob Type: The addition of Cob blood to the Welsh Pony has created a strong and reliable breed that make fine family ponies and solid jumpers. Size: Up to 13.2 h.h.

The Highland: A good, strong all-round Scottish pony suitable for the family and trekking. Size: Up to 14.2 h.h.

The Shetland: Britain's smallest pony from islands off northern Scotland is usually kept as a novelty or as a first pony for a young child. Their rather comical appearance belies a somewhat unreliable and bad temperament. Size: Average 1m (3 ft 3 in).

The Welsh Mountain: An excellent and reliable children's pony, the Welsh Mountain is hardy, intelligent and good-looking, in part due to an early influx of Arab and Thoroughbred blood. Size: Up to 12 h.h.

The Welsh Pony: The traditional shepherd's pony, the Welsh Pony is sure-footed with a good temperament that makes it a good children's riding pony. Size: Up to 13.2 h.h.

The Welsh Pony – Cob Type: The addition of Cob blood to the Welsh Pony has created a strong and reliable breed that make fine family ponies and solid jumpers. Size: Up to 13.2 h.h.

The Highland: A good, strong all-round Scottish pony suitable for the family and trekking. Size: Up to 14.2 h.h.

The Shetland: Britain's smallest pony from islands off northern Scotland is usually kept as a novelty or as a first pony for a young child. Their rather comical appearance belies a somewhat unreliable and bad temperament. Size: Average 1m (3 ft 3 in)

COLOURS

Colour may be a factor in choosing your horse. If you are looking for Black Beauty you need to be aware that this will limit your choice as there are relatively few black horses overall to choose from. Horses of black, dun, roan or grey colour are not common among the majority of breeds.

Breed	Colour
APPALOOSA	Spotted coat, either dark spots on light background, or the opposite
CLYDESDALE	Bay, brown or grey
DALES	Black
DARTMOOR	Most colours
EXMOOR	Brown, bay or dun
FELL	Black
HIGHLAND	Black, brown, dun or grey
MORGAN	Bay, black, or chestnut
NEW FOREST	Any colour
PERCHERON	Black or grey
QUARTER HORSE	All solid colours, usually chestnut
SADDLEBRED	Bay, black, chestnut or grey
SHETLAND	Any colour
SHIRE	Any colour
STANDARD-BRED	Bay, black, or chestnut
SUFFOLK	Chestnut
TENNESSEE WALKING HORSE	Black or chestnut
WELSH COB	Any colour
WELSH MOUNTAIN	All whole colour, usually grey
WELSH PONY	Any colour
WELSH PONY – COB TYPE	Any colour

STOCKING   SOCK

The markings on a horse's legs and face are used to give it a physical description and are useful if the horse is stolen.

STAR AND SNIP   STRIPE   BLAZE   WHITE FACE

ABOVE: *Welsh mountain ponies carry Arab blood.*
RIGHT: *Shetland ponies on their native islands.*
BELOW: *The Welsh heavy cob is hard-working and reliable.*

THE AMERICAN BREEDS

The six major American breeds all find their origins in European stock and have been bred for racing, cattle-ranching, showing and all-round versatility.

The Morgan: With Arab, Thoroughbred and Welsh Cob breeding, the Morgan is a very popular breed. Being strong, versatile and good-natured, this breed is the perfect pleasure riding horse under either Western or English saddle and in harness. Size: Up to 15.3 h.h.

The Quarter Horse: A well-built horse with a good temperament, the Quarter Horse's compactness and agility made it ideal for herding cattle. It was developed through Spanish mares and English stallions. Still used in cattle-ranching, it is a good pleasure riding horse and is still sometimes raced. Size: Up to 15.3 h.h.

The Saddlebred: Developed from Morgan, Thoroughbred and Pacer stock, the Saddlebred has an easy-going temperament, good stamina and is a comfortable ride. It is bred mainly for the show ring where it is exhibited under saddle and in harness. Size: Up to 16 h.h.

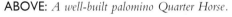

ABOVE: *A well-built palomino Quarter Horse.*
LEFT: *The spotted coat of the Appaloosa has made it a popular parade horse.*
RIGHT & ABOVE RIGHT: *Saddlebreds with their distinctive uplifted tails are bred mainly for showing.*

The Tennessee Walking Horse: Strong and powerful, but with a gentle nature, the Tennessee Walking Horse was bred as a general purpose working-horse and is one of America's favourite breeds. It has an unusual four-beat gait – each foot strikes the ground separately at regular intervals – which make it extremely comfortable to ride. Size: Up to 16 h.h.

The Appaloosa: Selectively bred by Native Americans from horses of Spanish stock. With its unique spotted coat, the Appaloosa is even-tempered, quick on its feet and makes a popular riding horse under both Western and English saddle. It is now bred throughout the world. Size: Up to 15.3 h.h.

The Standardbred: This breed traces its line back to a single Thoroughbred exported to the United States in 1788. Originally bred for flat-racing, the line evolved into the best trotting horses under saddle and now in harness. Strong, brave and staying, Standardbreds either pace or trot. Pacers move the front and hind legs on the same side together, trotters are described as 'diagonally gaited'. The method seems to be inherited. Size: Up to 15.5 h.h.

THE HEAVY BREEDS

The big heavy horses almost disappeared with the mechanization of agriculture and heavy draught transport, but today the breeds are being revived both to be shown and for work, either as dray horses or on the land. The British Shire is one of the biggest horses in the world, standing at up to 18 h.h. and a genuine gentle giant. The Suffolk is slightly smaller, as is the Clydesdale from Scotland. In France the Percheron at up to 17 h.h. is one of the more graceful heavy horses, partly due to its Arab ancestry. Other heavy breeds are found throughout France, Belgium and Holland, but they are generally stockier than their cousins.

Finally, there are recognized breeds from every country in the world from Iceland to New Zealand. Many have Arab or Thoroughbred blood-lines and are bred for a variety of working purposes as well as for showing, racing, dressage and eventing.

LEFT: *A champion British Shire at a heavy horse show.*
RIGHT: *A two-year-old French trotter.*
BELOW: *Icelandic ponies are closely related to the Shetland.*

Chapter 2
THE CARE AND MAINTENANCE OF TACK

Saddles, bridles and all their accessories are collectively known as tack.

It is essential that you have the right tack to fit your horse, that you know how

to fit it, and, as it is expensive, how to look after it properly.

THE TACK

SADDLES

The whole point of a saddle is to provide the rider with a more secure base than riding bareback and so means that the rider has more control of the horse. When choosing a saddle it should fit both horse and rider. For the horse's comfort the saddle must be wide enough to avoid pinching the spine and below the withers, and high enough to clear the withers by about 5 cm (2 in), or allow you to put three fingers between the withers and the pommel. The rider should be able to sit in the middle of the saddle without touching either the pommel or cantle, and it must be of the correct width so that the rider's leg muscles are not stretched. Saddles are made in a standard selection of widths and lengths and it is a question of selecting the correct combination.

Saddles, like horses, come with different features which suit them and their particular needs. Horse-racing saddles, for example,

ABOVE: *From the left: jumping, dressage and general purpose saddles.*
LEFT: *The tack room.*

THE DRESSAGE SADDLE

The dressage saddle is designed to push the rider's weight backwards towards the cantle and to expose the horse's shoulders. The stirrup bars are set further back and there are only two, rather than three, girth straps extending below the straight-cut flap.

NUMNAHS

Numnahs are saddle-shaped pads that fit under the saddle. They are made of sheepskin, synthetic sheepskin or fabric-covered foam in a variety of designs. While being attractive, they give added protection to the horse's back, especially if it has been clipped. It is important to wash the numnah after every time it is used.

differ greatly in size, weight and shape from everyday general riding saddles. There are basically three types of saddle – the general riding saddle, dressage and show-jumping. There are, however, only minor variations between them which mainly affect the height of the pommel and cantle, and the cut and angle of the flap.

Saddles are built on a frame, called the tree, and most have two metal springs at the back to make the ride more comfortable. The leather covering can be any colour and can be plain or decoratively tooled. Saddles also have knee-rolls which support the knees and thighs of the rider.

GIRTHS AND STIRRUPS

The saddle is held in place by a girth which buckles onto straps under the main saddle flap and can be adjusted for length. The most common are an even strip about 8 cm (3 in) wide made of fabric or woven nylon which is less likely to stretch in wet weather than traditional leather. Variations include the Atherstone and the Balding which are narrower in the middle part where they sit behind the horse's elbows. The Atherstone has an extra strip of leather running down the middle, while the Balding is divided into three strips with the outer two plaited around the central one. These kinds of girth are usually chosen if the horse is sensitive to chafing.

The stirrup irons are attached by stirrup leathers to the saddle, and these in turn are hooked onto a metal clip at the top of the skirt and adjusted for length by a buckle. The clips are designed as a safety feature so if a rider falls and his foot gets stuck in the stirrup iron, the leather will slip off to prevent the rider being dragged along. Some saddles have a surcingle loop to hold the extra length of the leathers. Modern stirrup irons are no longer made of actual iron, but of stainless steel or nickel. Stainless steel irons are slightly more expensive, but they are stronger and will last longer.

The most usual stirrup iron is called the plain iron, which can be fitted with a rubber pad to prevent the foot slipping. Always choose an iron big enough to ensure that your foot cannot become jammed in it if you fall. Other stirrup irons include the Kournakoff which has an upward-sloping tread to keep the rider's heel down and toe up, and offset holes for the leathers. The Peacock, or child's safety stirrup, has a tread that is suspended on strong elastic sides, so that if the rider falls, the foot cannot be trapped and slips out of the stirrup more easily.

BITS

The metal bit which is fitted into the horse's mouth is one of the means by which the rider controls the horse, changes direction and stops. There are various designs which have evolved from

TIPS

★ Change over your stirrup leathers to the other side of the saddle every now and then as the near-side leather will tend to stretch more as it takes your weight when mounting.

★ If your saddle continually slides backwards use a breastplate to help hold it in position. This consists of a band across the horse's chest and a narrower strap over its shoulders that is attached to the saddle. You should also consider finding another saddle, one which fits your horse. Generally, the less tack you have to use at one time, the better the riding experience for both yourself and your mount.

★ Saddle covers with elasticated edges easily fit over the saddle and keep it clean and dry if you are tacking up outdoors. If you are spending a day at a show, a saddle cover can also be used to keep the saddle dry if the weather is bad.

SADDLES

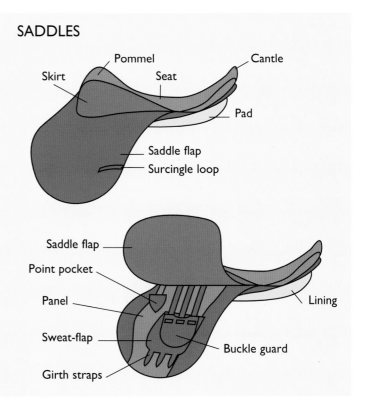

ABOVE: *Make the final adjustment to the girth when mounted.*

traditional forms over hundreds of years and they exercise differing amounts of control depending on what the horse needs. The most widely used bit, and the mildest, is called the snaffle, of which there are several variations. The mouthpiece can be curved, straight or jointed and in various thicknesses. Generally, the thicker the mouthpiece the less severe the action. A jointed mouthpiece is the hardest as the two halves squeeze across the lower jaw. The bit rings, to which the reins are attached, can be loose or fixed. If they are loose, the bit must be broad enough so that the rings do not pinch the corners of the mouth.

The pelham has a more severe action and is often used for strong ponies. Like the snaffle, there are several variations. The pelham is

designed to be used with two reins and has two bit rings at the top and bottom on each side. If the rider has difficulty handling two reins then couplers can be used. These consist of two leather straps joined to the bit rings which are then connected to a single rein.

Other bit arrangements should only be used by experienced riders and can be quite severe in order to control a headstrong horse. If a horse or pony needs this much control then it is certainly not suitable for young children or beginners. The double bridle has two bits and two sets of reins which are used independently. The two bits are called the bridoon – which acts like a snaffle bit – and the curb which is a straight bar with a curved bridge in the middle to clear the tongue. In addition there

BITS IN ACTION

All bits are designed to put pressure on a part of the horse's head and/or mouth.

SNAFFLE Upwards on the corners of the mouth

PELHAM Upwards on the corners of the mouth, downwards on the tongue bars, curb groove and poll

DOUBLE BRIDLE Upwards on the corners of the mouth, downwards on the bars, curb groove and poll

GAG   Upwards on the corners of the mouth, downwards on the poll

BITLESS   Downwards on the nose, poll and curb groove

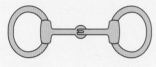

SNAFFLE BIT

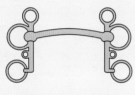

PELHAM BIT

DOUBLE BRIDLE BIT

BITLESS BRIDLE OR HACKAMORE

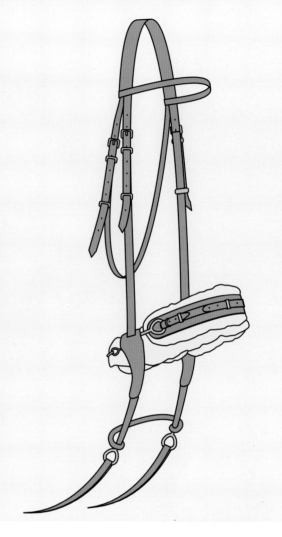

is a curb chain and a lip strap to keep the curb chain in place. The curb chain is a metal-linked chain that hooks onto both sides of the mouthpiece.

The gag bit is very severe and should only be used as a last resort to control a horse – and then only by very experienced riders. In essence it is a snaffle bit with two reins. The first rein controls the snaffle in the normal way and acts on the mouth, the second rein, called the gag rein, causes the bit to be pulled up the cheekpieces of the bridle, exerting upward pressure on the horse's mouth and the top of the bridle on the horse's head.

Another control system is the bitless bridle (called a hackamore or scawbrig) which has no bit at all. Pressure is exerted through the padded noseband which is levered downwards by specially designed plates attached to a single rein. Although the bitless

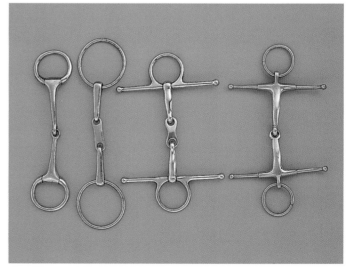

ABOVE: *Bridoon, Loose ring snaffle, Cheek snaffle, Fulmer.*
RIGHT: *Snaffle bridle with flash noseband.*

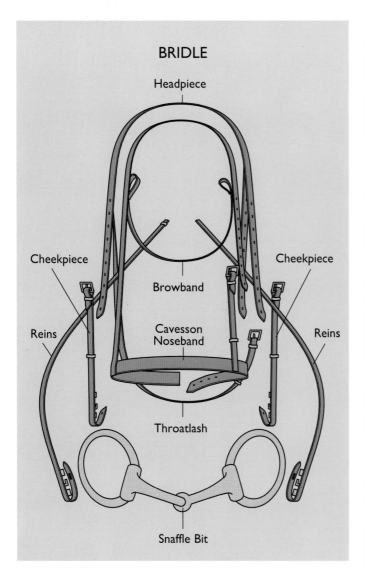

BRIDLE

Headpiece

Cheekpiece

Cheekpiece

Browband

Reins

Cavesson
Noseband

Reins

Throatlash

Snaffle Bit

bridle may sound gentle, its action can be quite severe and needs experienced riders to use it. It is, however, suitable for a horse with an injured mouth or one that has been ruined by bad riding and the mouth is insensitive.

BRIDLES

Whatever bit you use, the bridle will be the same, only varying in size to make a good fit on the horse's head. The parts of the bridle are the headpiece, throatlash, browband, cheekpieces, noseband and reins.

The headpiece sits behind the horse's ears and is buckled to the cheekpieces which run alongside the horse's cheeks and are attached to the bit rings. The browband fits onto the headpiece and is set in front of the horse's ears. Browbands are often decorated with brass studs or coloured embroidery. The throatlash is a thin leather strap that passes under the horse's

ABOVE: *A pelham bit with curb chain.*
RIGHT: *A double bridle can be used to control a headstrong horse.*

TACKING UP

THE SADDLE

STEP ONE: Carry the saddle on your left forearm with the pommel nearest your left elbow. The stirrup irons should be run up and the girth buckled on the off-side and draped back over the saddle towards you.

STEP TWO: Put on the saddle from the near-side, in front of the withers and slide it back into position.

STEP THREE: Reach under the horse and catch the girth, which has been left to hang free on the opposite side, and fasten gently, but firmly, so the saddle does not slip from position. Give the girth a final tightening as far as possible just before mounting.

THE BRIDLE

STEP ONE: Carry the bridle by the headpiece and the loop of the reins.

STEP TWO: Standing on the near-side, place the reins over the horse's head and remove the head collar or fasten loosely around the neck.

STEP THREE: Place your right hand either midway on the horse's nose or place your right arm between the horse's ears with the top of the bridle in hand. Present the bit to the horse's mouth, ideally with the bit balanced on top of your thumb and third finger spread to either side of the horse's mouth. If the horse refuses to open his mouth, press your fingers on either side of the large spaces between the horse's forward and rear teeth and press until the mouth opens. Insert the bit and pull the headpiece over the ears.

STEP FOUR: Check the position of the headpiece behind the horse's ears. Fasten the cavesson as required and buckle the throatlash so it flops easily against the horse's upper jaw. Leave room to insert two fingers under the cavesson and four fingers under the throatlash. Tuck the horse's forelock under the headband if desired, but above all, make sure that the horse is as comfortable as he can be in the bridle.

When the rider is mounted the girth should be tightened a hole or two and the stirrup leathers adjusted for length. The correct length is for the stirrup tread to be level with the rider's ankle when the leg is allowed to hang down naturally out of the iron.

SAFETY FIRST!

It is not just the horse that should be tacked up properly. The rider must be appropriately kitted out for safety and comfort. The first essential is a well-fitted, design-approved hard riding hat, which must be worn at all times. Never buy a secondhand one as it may be cracked or damaged, even if you cannot see the problem. Padded back protectors, which strap onto the rider's back and are worn under a jacket, are a good idea if you are jumping or hacking out. Even the most experienced rider takes a fall occasionally.

Trousers or jodhpurs should not have raised seams as these rub on the inside of the thighs, and especially the knees, quickly causing quite severe chafing. Riding boots protect the calves. Rubber riding boots, rather than leather, are a practical everyday solution as they can be cleaned quickly and easily by hosing them down. There is nothing worse than being cold and wet on horseback. Warm clothing, a waterproof jacket and even riding gloves should be part of the rider's wardrobe.

throat to ensure that the bridle cannot slip over the horse's head. The noseband circles the horse's nose to prevent it opening its mouth too widely and is held in place by a strap that buckles to the headpiece. The reins are attached to the bit rings.

There are various different nosebands, but the most common is the cavesson which has more of an aesthetic than practical purpose. Other nosebands, such as the drop, the flash and the grackle, have a specific purpose, which is to keep the horse's mouth closed so that it cannot cross or open its jaws in an attempt to avoid the bit.

Reins can be made of leather, nylon or webbing and are plaited, braided or plain. Some have a rubber grip or V-shaped pieces of leather which help the rider keep a better grip in wet weather.

MARTINGALES

A martingale is used on horses that carry their heads too high in an attempt to avoid the bit and lessen a rider's control. There are two commonly used kinds – the standing and the running. The standing martingale is attached to the underside of a cavesson noseband and the girth, with a neck strap to hold it in place. This puts pressure on the horse's nose if it throws its head up. When positioned correctly the standing martingale should form a straight line between the girth and noseband when the horse's head is held at the right height.

The running martingale has two straps that run from the girth to the reins and are then threaded through the rings. When the horse's head and the rider's hands are in the right position the martingale should be adjusted so that the reins run in a straight

ABOVE: *A polo-pony being cooled down between chukkas.*

line from hands to bit. The running martingale pulls on the horse's mouth if it lifts its head.

The so-called Irish martingale is not really a martingale at all, but a device to prevent the reins coming over the horse's head if the rider falls. It comprises a short strip of leather with rings through which the reins pass and is set just behind the bit.

Two other pieces of useful stable equipment are a head collar and leading rein. The head collar is used as an alternative to a bridle when leading the horse or for securing it when grooming, travelling, shoeing and being examined by a veterinarian. They are available in smart leather, but most usually they are made of woven nylon which is very strong and long-lasting. The leading rein clips onto the head collar and is useful for leading the horse in hand, especially if you are walking it to dry it off after a bath, or for keeping control of the horse if a beginner or youngster is riding.

CARING FOR TACK

All tack should be cleaned regularly and thoroughly. Mud and dirt from the fields and sweat and grease from the horse collect on the tack and if not cleaned off, will harden into lumps that will rub the horse's skin. Regular cleaning makes life easier as it is simpler to clean off new dirt than caked dirt that has accumulated over a period of weeks.

Dismantle the bridle completely to clean every part on both sides. Strip down the saddle by removing the girth, stirrup irons and stirrup leathers. Use a damp sponge and warm water to wipe down the leather, loosening and removing all the dirt. Allow the leather to dry before rubbing in saddle soap with a damp sponge. Vigorous rubbing will produce a shine. Non-leather girths should be washed and scrubbed and allowed to dry.

From time to time, all the leather should be oiled or greased to soften it and prevent it cracking, especially if it is stored for periods and unused. Equally, new leather should be oiled before it is used.

The stirrup irons and bit should be washed to remove any deposits, especially saliva on the bit. The bit rings and stirrup irons can be polished with a proprietary metal polish or rubbed down with a fine grade of wire wool. If using metal polish on the bit, do not forget to wash and dry it afterwards as the horse may reject an unfamiliar and unpleasant taste. When everything is dry the saddle and bridle should be reassembled. The saddle should be stored on a saddle rack with the girth buckled to the off-side and draped back over the saddle. The stirrup irons should be run up the leathers and fitted under the skirt. The bridle should be hung up with the reins through the throatlash.

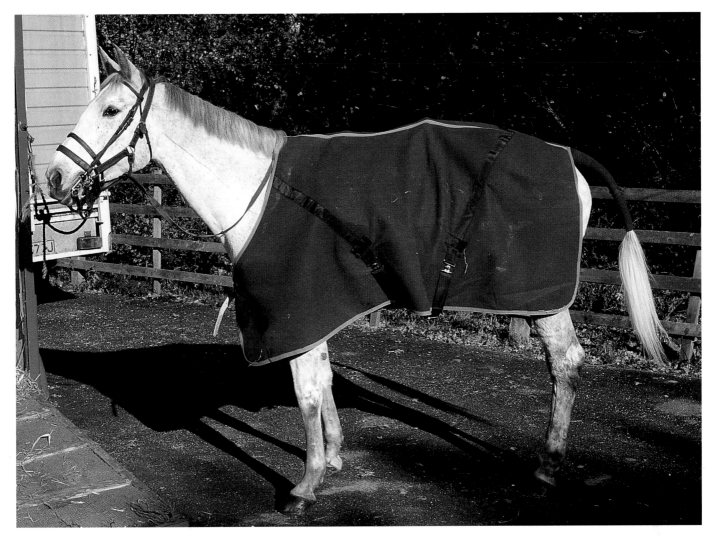

ABOVE: *A day blanket keeps the horse warm when travelling.*
LEFT: *Back protectors can save the rider from severe injuries.*

Keep a regular check on the condition of the leather for signs of wear and tear or loose stitching. Repairs should be undertaken by a professional saddler, sooner rather than later.

OTHER THINGS YOU WILL NEED

In addition to the tack, there are other pieces of equipment you will need. Rugs, blankets and protective clothing are all necessary, and essential if a horse is travelling in a box to a show or event.

RUGS AND BLANKETS

Horses, like people, need some protection from the cold to keep them in good condition. Even a stabled horse will need to wear a night rug when the weather is cold, especially if it has been clipped. Today, rugs are made in a variety of materials, although they were traditionally jute or canvas with a woollen lining. Modern materials are lighter and easier to keep clean, the most common being made of polyester-filled nylon with a soft lining. Some have detachable linings and a waterproof covering which means they can be used both in the stable and when the horse is turned out during the day. Rugs are also useful to keep the horse clean the night before a show so that bathing and grooming can be done in advance.

Turned out horses usually wear the more hard-wearing and protective New Zealand rug which is made of heavy waterproof canvas with a felt or woollen lining. These rugs have adjustable straps which fit around the horse's back legs to prevent it slipping or coming off when the horse rolls or rubs against trees and fences. Horses, however, have a remarkable capacity to disturb their rugs and they need to have them adjusted regularly.

Sweat blankets are lightweight and made of a meshed cellular material like a huge string vest. They are used after the horse has

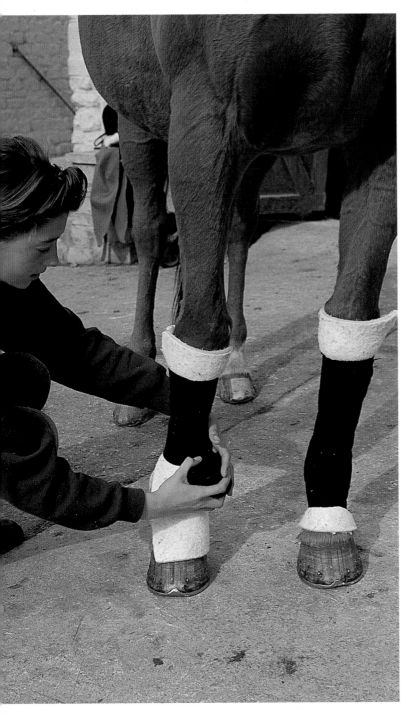

LEFT: *Stable bandages protect the legs from knocks.*
RIGHT: *An American Quarter Horse in full Western tack.*

can be wound over gamgee cotton wool wadding from knee to coronet. Hock boots and knee pads can be used on a horse that tends to bang its hocks and knees. All-in-one travelling boots are also available and simple to use. They are made from foam-covered synthetic materials and fasten at the back with Velcromesh straps. Tail bandages not only keep the tail clean but also prevent the horse rubbing it against the trailer door.

Even when exercising, during general riding and jumping, some horses have a tendency to knock their legs. Elasticated bandages over cotton wool wadding should be wound from the knee to the fetlock. Horses can also kick themselves, and brushing boots will protect the fetlocks. Over-reach boots are circular rubber or plastic cups that fit over the hooves – they are particularly useful for show-jumpers whose hind legs kick the forelegs when landing.

WESTERN TACK

Tack for Western-style riding is, in principle, the same as any other – all use a saddle and bridle. The differences of design, however, have evolved for two reasons: first, there is a strong Spanish influence and, secondly, Western tack was designed for comfort when working with cattle which involves long, hard days in the saddle.

The Western saddle differs from its English counterpart in several respects. It is flatter and wider, has a high cantle and prominent pommel which is further modified by the extension of the horn, which is used to secure the rope, or lariat, when roping cattle. The stirrup leathers are wider, pushing the rider's legs away from the horse's sides and the stirrups themselves are made of wood covered with leather. The saddle is always worn with one or more blankets underneath and the girth is known as a cinch, a term derived from the Spanish. A second cinch is sometimes added to the back of the saddle to hold it in place when roping cattle because the lariat tied to the horn has a tendency to draw the saddle forward.

Generally, the reins are split so that when the rider dismounts they drop to the ground, signalling to the horse that it should stand still. This is a technique derived from the need for the rider to dismount quickly when roping cattle and is known as 'ground hitching'.

exercised to allow it to dry off without becoming cold, just as an athlete puts on a tracksuit after competing. Day rugs are useful for two purposes – to keep the horse warm when travelling and when spending time waiting for the next class at a show. It also keeps the coat free of dirt, dust and disturbance.

LEG PROTECTORS

A horse's legs are its most vulnerable points and when travelling they will need to be protected from knocks in the box. Bandages

Chapter 3
CARING FOR YOUR HORSE

Caring for your horse is more than simply riding it, although naturally regular

exercise is important to keep it fit. Looking after a horse means, among other things,

providing food and shelter, grooming, shoeing and general health care. While some

horses seem to fend for themselves, others — especially if they have Arab or

Thoroughbred blood — need a lot more attention.

THE HORSE'S BASIC NEEDS

FEEDING

Horses need food for the same reason as humans: general health, growth and energy to work. A young, growing horse, or one that is active and worked hard, has a greater requirement of energy than one that is turned out to graze most of the time.

A horse that does little work can be turned out and left to feed on good grass in summer and be given hay and high-protein feed supplements in winter. A pony or small horse will need at least

HAY-NETS

Hay-nets are the safest way to feed a stabled or boxed horse hay as long as you make sure the hay-net is tied securely and that it is high enough to prevent the horse being able to paw it and catch its hooves in the netting.

LEFT: *A stabled horse needs to be able to look out to be happy.*
RIGHT: *Weighing the hay-net ensures the correct amount.*

ABOVE: *A selection of feedstuffs: sugar beet, maize, barley and oats.*

RIGHT: *Holstein mares in the snow.*

0.5 hectares (1 acre) of good grass, and preferably more, to have enough natural food without the need for supplementary feeding. If the pasture is poor, or the area smaller, it is essential to manage the feeding carefully. To keep the pasture lush it may be necessary to dress it with lime and fertilizers regularly, depending on the kind of soil. The pasture should be kept clear of invasive weeds which reduce the horse's grazing area and poisonous weeds must be removed whenever found. In winter, the horse's diet will need to be supplemented with hay and other food.

For the stabled horse the picture is very different. It will need to be fed every day with a balance of bulk fibre food, such as hay, and supplementary food that provides adequate levels of protein, fats, carbohydrates, vitamins and minerals. The exact balance and amount is hard to specify as this will depend on the individual needs of the horse and the amount of work that it does each day and week. Generally, a horse that is worked every day will need equal measures of bulk and concentrate food – and the more work they do, the more energy from the concentrates they need. However, a horse should never be fed on only concentrate food, and at least a third of the diet should be made up of bulk food.

Bulk foods are grass, hay, carrots and bran, while concentrate foods such as barley, maize and oats are high in fats and carbohydrates. Both kinds provide varying amounts of protein, vitamins and salts. Proprietary, ready-mixed horse food is available from feed merchants and has a balanced ration which saves the owner from mixing up the ingredients themselves.

WATER

A horse will drink up to 45 litres (10 gallons) of water a day, and half as much again in hot weather. It is essential that a horse, whether turned out or stabled, has access to an unlimited supply of water. Buckets are not always practical as a horse will drink a

bucketful in one go and they are all too easily knocked over. Unless you are lucky enough to have a stream with easy access for the horse, the best solution is a trough that is connected to the mains supply and fed by an automatic valve. Otherwise it will need to be topped up regularly by hose or bucket. In the stable, a drinking bowl should be provided, ideally one that self-fills.

In winter, when there are heavy frosts, the water trough should be checked daily to make sure that it has not frozen over. An old tennis ball left to float on the surface will keep it clear to a certain extent, otherwise the ice will have to be broken up.

THE TURNED OUT HORSE

Whether permanently turned out, or turned out for part of the day, a horse will need some kind of shelter to protect it from wind and rain all year round, and the attention of insects in summer. A field shelter should be large enough for several horses and have one open side facing north so that it does not receive sun. A hay-rack, or rings for attaching hay-nets, should be fitted on the inside so that the horse can be fed in the dry in winter. A salt lick kept inside will also help to discourage the horse from chewing trees and fencing if it is short of minerals.

LEFT: *Field-kept horses need protection from sun in summer.*

RIGHT: *Freeze marking for security.*

FAR RIGHT: *A grey Arabian mare poses for the camera.*

SECURITY

For horses, the grass on the other side of the fence is very often literally greener, and they will escape from their field at any opportunity. Even the well-fed ones will do it for devilment if the opportunity arises. Secure fencing and gates are essential and they should be checked weekly for signs of weakness. Posts and rails are the best, but most expensive, solution. Heavy gauge wire strung between posts is the most cost-effective method but ensure that the bottom wire is at least 30 cm (12 in) from the ground to prevent the horse catching its feet. Never use barbed wire because if it slackens off – which it usually does – a horse can become caught in it and injure itself.

Hedges provide shelter from wind and rain where fences do not and this provides a more natural environment for the animals. A hedge, however, also needs to be maintained because gaps may appear when trees or shrubs die or are damaged. Equally, it will need to be fairly mature and strong enough to prevent escape. Like the paddock, hedges should be checked for poisonous plants.

Gates must be strong and well-hinged so that they are easy to open and close both from the ground and the saddle. They should be padlocked and chained, at both the opening and hinged ends, to prevent anybody from being able to rustle the horse. Horse stealing is sadly more common than is usually realized or admitted.

Security tagging the horse is a worthwhile idea. Freeze-marking involves using a freeze brand that destroys the colour pigments in the horse's hair. The bald patch grows back with white hair within a few weeks. The numbers and letters will be registered as belonging to your horse and you will receive documentation to prove it. The mark is usually made on the back of the horse and is covered by the saddle whenever it is tacked up. High-tech versions of tagging, involving the implanting of a microchip, are now also available. Both methods are painless.

When a horse is turned out, it is relatively self-sufficient in food and water, but this does not mean that it can look after itself entirely. Even the hardiest of native ponies need some form of attention. The horse should be visited every day to have its feet picked out and checked over for knocks and scratches.

Again, depending on the breed, a day rug or overnight New Zealand rug will have to be fitted as needed. These should be checked at least twice a day to make sure that they have not slipped or the straps are rubbing.

Another regular tasks is worming every six or eight weeks, especially if the field is small and the danger of parasites consequently greater.

SHOEING

The horse's feet should be checked at least every six weeks, and preferably every four. The horn of a horse's hoof is continually growing from the top of the hoof, producing about 2.5 cm (1 in)

each month. A horse out at grass may be able to manage without shoes as the horn is worn down at the same rate as it grows, but any horse worked on hard surfaces will need to be shod, otherwise the horn will be worn away, leading to lameness.

Whether a horse is shod or not, the hooves will need to be trimmed regularly to prevent the hoof wall cracking and splitting. Equally, uneven wear due to the horse's conformation (a horse with legs that turn outwards, for example, wears down the inner walls more quickly) needs to be corrected, otherwise the conformation problems become worse and place undue strain on the tendons. Trimming also maintains the correct alignment of the hoof and pastern. Although the toe horn grows faster than the heel, a horse at grass is likely to wear down the toes more quickly

LEFT: *Mare and foal in stable with straw bedding.*
RIGHT: *American-style barn stables allow all chores to be carried out in the dry.*
BELOW: *A horse may need to be shod every six weeks.*

THE HORSE NEEDS SHOEING WHEN:

★ The shoe is thin and worn
★ The shoe is loose
★ A shoe has been cast
★ The clenches are standing proud of the hoof

POISONOUS PLANTS

Some plants and trees are poisonous to horses and should be removed from hedges and pastures. These include:

Bryony	Deadly Nightshade
Hemlock	Laburnum
Privet	Ragwort
St John's Wort	Yew

SWEETS AND TREATS

All horses and ponies enjoy extra treats such as apples, bread and carrots. Peppermints are popular and some horses are as addicted to cola-type drinks as many children. When feeding with apples it is essential that they are crushed first or the whole apple may catch in the horse's throat and choke it.

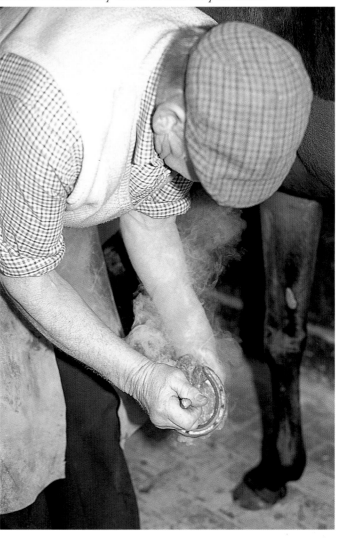

and the heel will need to be trimmed. A shod horse tends to wear the heel horn as there is more friction when it moves, so the toes will need to be trimmed more often.

Shoeing must be carried out by a qualified farrier who will use one of two methods – hot shoeing or cold shoeing. First, the old clenches, or fixing nails, are cut and the old shoe is levered off with pincers. Overgrown horn is then trimmed with a drawing knife. When hot shoeing, the shoe is forged to fit the hoof exactly and applied hot. This will reveal any unevenness which is then trimmed down before the shoe is fixed with the clenches. The clenches are then smoothed off with a rasp. In cold shoeing, the shoes are pre-cast and fitted cold. Whichever method is used, it is important that the shoe fits the hoof rather than the hoof being trimmed to fit the shoe.

THE STABLED HORSE

A stable can be constructed of almost any building material as long as it is secure, warm, has good air circulation, a concrete floor, adequate drainage and is of the correct size. A horse may be in its stable for 22 hours a day and must be comfortable. The stable should be at least 4.5 m (14 ft) by 3.8 m (12 ft) for a horse and slightly smaller for a pony. The ceiling must be high enough both to prevent the horse from banging its head and to allow air to circulate. It is essential that the horse has room to move easily and can lie down and get up without any problems.

Usually stable doors are of a split variety, the bottom half securely bolted at its top and bottom on the outside, while the upper half is left open to allow air to circulate and light to come in. The

hay and bedding. A secure tack room is also useful if the stable is some distance from where you live.

STABLE ROUTINE

The stabled horse needs to be looked after every day and a basic stable routine takes up an enormous amount of time and can never be missed. It begins early in the morning and finishes in early evening. The first thing to do in the morning is to check the horse for any damage or injuries that it may have inflicted on itself during the night, and to adjust the night blanket if it has slipped. The horse will then need to be fed and the drinking water replaced.

The next job is to muck out the stable: remove all the bedding material and droppings and replace with fresh bedding. Bedding comes in a variety of materials, straw being the most usual. Use wheat straw as a rule, and avoid both barley and oat straw because barley can irritate the horse's skin and horses tend to eat oat straw. Alternative bedding materials are peat, sawdust, wood shavings and shredded paper (the last of which is particularly useful if the horse is allergic to straw).

Straw comes in tightly packed bales and needs to be teased apart and separated into a nice springy bed by hand or with a pitchfork. The entire floor should be covered and the straw banked up at the sides of the stable both to prevent draughts and to afford some protection to the horse as it moves during the night.

The deep-litter method of bedding is perhaps more practical as it is less time-consuming – but still needs to be done every day. Wet straw and droppings are removed each morning and new clean straw added. The level of the bed gradually rises and each week the entire bedding is removed and replaced.

After mucking out, the horse should be turned out for exercising, either to roam the paddock or to be ridden. The evening routine is similar. Droppings should be removed and the straw fluffed up. The horse should be fed and fresh water supplied, its hooves picked out, its coat groomed and the night blanket fitted.

EXERCISE

Stabled horses need regular exercise to keep them fit, stop them becoming bored and difficult, and to ensure that they give a good ride. There is no fixed exercise routine as it will depend on the

door should be at least 1.2 m (4 ft) wide to prevent the horse banging itself when entering or leaving, and the lower half should be high enough to prevent escape, but not so high that the horse cannot look out and amuse itself. Windows should be set high in the stable and covered on the inside with a protective wire grill.

Inside the stable you will need a manger for food, a drinking-water supply – either a self-filling system or a frame for a bucket to prevent the horse from turning it over – and a fixed ring to tie the horse to when grooming. This will also double as a position to fix a hay-net. Alternatively, a metal hay-rack can be fitted in one of the corners. A salt lick provides the minerals the horse needs and can help to stop the horse biting at any wood in the stable. Any lights and electrical cables must be sited out of the horse's reach and all switches must be on the outside of the stable.

Besides a stable to accommodate the horse, you will have to consider having a dry, vermin-proof store for the horse's food,

breed and size of the horse and the kind of work it will be expected to do. A hunter, for example, needs more exercise than a native pony. One basic rule is never to exercise a horse until an hour and a half after a heavy feed and keep the hay-net away for at least an hour beforehand.

GROOMING

Grooming is more than a way of making a horse look attractive – it also helps to keep the horse healthy, tones up muscle, and improves circulation and the condition of its coat. Most horses also enjoy the attention.

Stabled horses will need to be groomed every day before exercise. A light groom, known as quartering, removes dirt and dust with a body brush, concentrating on the areas that are underneath the saddle, girth and bridle. The mane and tail should

be straightened with a body and water brush and the eyes, nostrils and dock wiped with separate damp sponges. After exercising, the horse should be allowed to dry off before being given a thorough grooming, called strapping. First, pick out the hooves and then work on the coat proceeding from ears to tail, initially on the near-side and then on the off. Remove sweat and mud with either a plastic curry comb or a dandy brush, but do not use these on the head as they are too harsh. The softer body brush should be used here.

The hard work begins with the body brush. This must be used firmly if it is to have any effect. Brush the mane to the 'wrong side' to remove any scurf and dust in the roots and then brush the forelock. Work the body brush in a circular motion on the body, ending in the direction of the hairs with a flick to push the dust away. The metal curry comb, held in the other hand, is used to clean the body brush when it becomes clogged. Be gentle when

THE ESSENTIAL GROOMING KIT

All grooming kit should be kept tidy in a specially designed box or wire basket. Labelling each item with the name of either yourself or your horse helps to prevent losing things. Each horse should have its own grooming kit so that infections are not passed between different animals.

Dandy brush	Removes dried mud and sweat
Body brush	Removes dust and scurf
Water brush	Used on mane, tail and hooves
Rubber curry comb	Removes mud and dried sweat (and can be used as the metal curry comb, see below)
Metal curry comb	Used to clean body brush, never the horse
Mane comb	Used when trimming or plaiting mane or tail
Sweat scraper	Removes sweat and water
Sponges	One is used on the eyes, nostrils and lips, the other on the dock
Stable rubber	For the final polish of the coat
Hoof oil and brush	Shines up the hooves and prevents cracking
Hoof pick	Removes dirt and other objects from hoof

ABOVE: *Body brush and curry comb.*
RIGHT: *Picking out the horse's hoof.*

grooming the head, especially around the sensitive parts of nostrils, eyes and ears. Finish up by brushing the tail a few strands at a time to remove all knots and tangles.

Clean eyes, nostrils, lips and dock with the damp sponges, lay the mane and tail and clean the hooves with the water brush. Brush the hooves with hoof oil when they are dry. For the final finish, use the stable rubber – dampened and folded into a flat parcel – all over the coat, polishing in the same direction as the hairs of the coat, to remove the very last traces of dust.

At the end of day, a quick going over with a body brush before a night blanket is fitted is all that is needed.

Turned out horses need less grooming than stabled horses as they need a certain amount of grease in their coat to keep them warm

ABOVE: *Cleaning out the horse's eyes with a damp sponge.*

ABOVE: *Keep your grooming kit labelled and tidy.*

PICKING OUT FEET

Stand facing towards the horse's tail and run your hand down from its shoulder to its fetlock, encouraging it to put its weight on the other foot. Hold the pastern with the inner hand and lift up the foot, with the fetlock resting on your thigh above your knee.

Work the hoof pick from the frog to the toe, beginning by cleaning out the edges with the point to remove all mud and pebbles. Take care not to push the point into the frog.

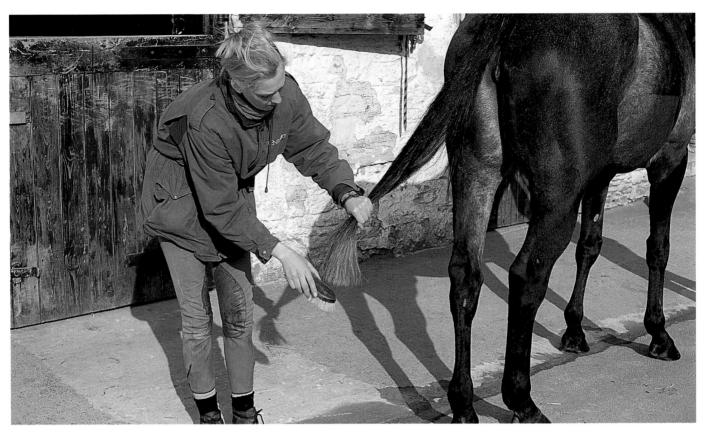

ABOVE: *Grooming a horse's tail that has been neatly clipped to hock level.*

and repel moisture. Vigorous brushing will remove the natural grease. They will, however, need to have their winter coat brushed out with a curry comb as the weather warms up and they begin to moult.

Grass-kept horses also tend to roll a lot, covering themselves with mud. In itself, dried mud does no harm at all, but if it becomes wet again it irritates the skin and causes chafing which can lead to skin infections. Continual washing of the horse will strip out the natural water-repellent grease so it is best to brush out the mud when it is dry. It is essential to remove all mud and dirt that is sited under the tack before riding. After exercise allow the horse to cool off, and the mud to dry, before grooming.

CLIPPING

If a horse is expected to work hard during winter, then clipping of the winter coat prevents it sweating too much or over-heating. There are different kinds of clip, depending on the amount of work the horse will do. None, however, should be done until the winter coat has fully grown in autumn and again in the New Year. If the horse is clipped it will need to wear a rug in the stable or a New Zealand rug if it is turned out during the day. Grass-kept horses should not be clipped.

The full clip is reserved for horses that undertake strenuous exercise, such as racehorses, but the most usual is the trace clip. The trace clip entails removing the coat from the underside of the neck, the stomach, the chest, and the fore and hind thighs. Hair is left on the legs. The blanket clip removes the hair from the head and neck, but leaves hair on the legs and across the back where a blanket would lie. The hunter clip leaves hair on the legs and a saddle-shaped patch on the back and flanks.

MANES AND TAILS

A horse's tail is designed so that it can keep its hind quarters free from flies and other biting insects and should be kept long. It can, however, be tidied by trimming it level with the hock. If the hairs thicken around the root of the tail and become regularly soiled, these can be plucked out singly or in twos or threes by wrapping them around a tail comb and pulling sharply. Bandaging also helps to tidy a tail, but make sure you dampen the tail before you start, as this makes the bandaging process easier. Do not, however, leave the tail bandage on overnight.

A thick, untidy mane that does not lie flat can also be plucked or pulled by removing the longest hairs from underneath. An evenly-pulled mane also helps to ensure that plaits are even.

CLIPPING

In late summer to early autumn, a horse will begin to grow a coarser and rougher winter coat. Clipping removes all or part of this coat to reduce sweating during exercise.

The new coat should become established before you clip, sometime in October. A second clip may be needed in late January as the coat continues to grow.

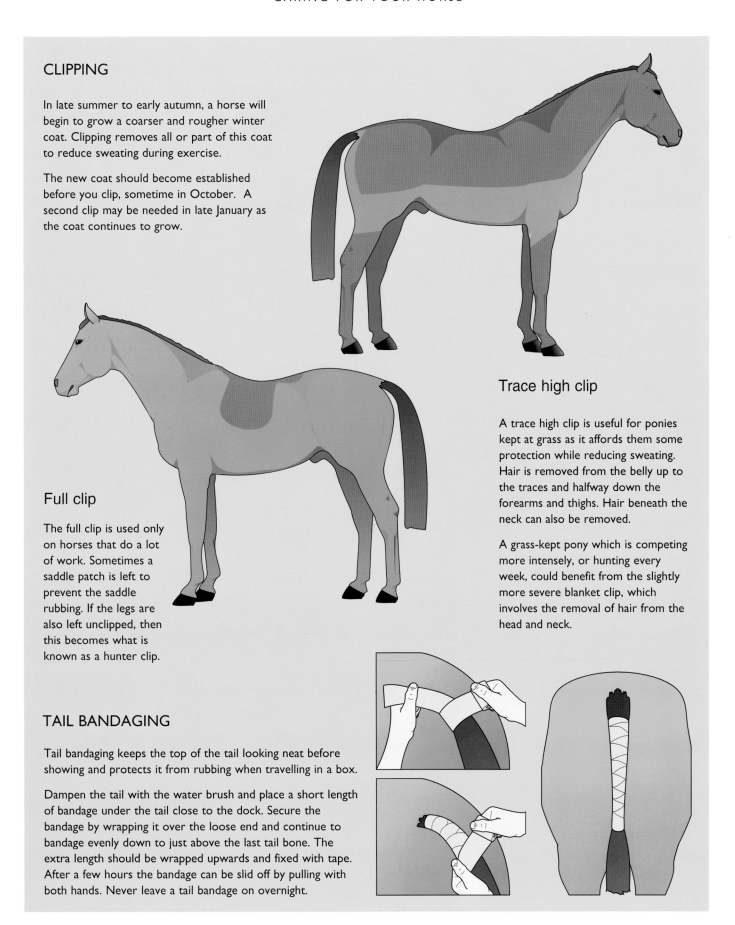

Trace high clip

A trace high clip is useful for ponies kept at grass as it affords them some protection while reducing sweating. Hair is removed from the belly up to the traces and halfway down the forearms and thighs. Hair beneath the neck can also be removed.

A grass-kept pony which is competing more intensely, or hunting every week, could benefit from the slightly more severe blanket clip, which involves the removal of hair from the head and neck.

Full clip

The full clip is used only on horses that do a lot of work. Sometimes a saddle patch is left to prevent the saddle rubbing. If the legs are also left unclipped, then this becomes what is known as a hunter clip.

TAIL BANDAGING

Tail bandaging keeps the top of the tail looking neat before showing and protects it from rubbing when travelling in a box.

Dampen the tail with the water brush and place a short length of bandage under the tail close to the dock. Secure the bandage by wrapping it over the loose end and continue to bandage evenly down to just above the last tail bone. The extra length should be wrapped upwards and fixed with tape. After a few hours the bandage can be slid off by pulling with both hands. Never leave a tail bandage on overnight.

Chapter 4
TRAINING

Regular training for both horse and rider will increase your enjoyment of riding.

By training together, you learn together, and create that special bond that will

allow you to develop your confidence and competence.

TRAINING THE RIDER

As in all sports, some people have a natural ability while others must practise and train hard to develop their skills, and the same is true in horse-riding. Riding, however, is both sport and recreation and it is not necessary to achieve a high standard of competence to be able to enjoy the pleasure of sitting astride a horse. It makes little difference to one's ultimate enjoyment whether you are hacking through the countryside or facing a 1 m (3 ft) fence.

If you do hope to become an accomplished rider however, it is as important to train yourself as it is to train your mount. A good rider can make up for many faults in a horse's training, but a well-trained horse can never compensate for a poor rider.

WHAT MAKES A GOOD RIDER?

There are four basic characteristics which every good rider needs: fitness, flexibility, balance and attitude.

To the casual observer it may seem that in horse-riding it is the horse who does all the work with the person on top merely 'coming along for the ride'. The truth is that a good rider needs to be fit, with good muscle tone in the legs – particularly the thighs – stomach and back. These are the main areas used to

LEFT: *An Hungarian show-jumper safely over.*

maintain a tight seat, leaving you in a position to control the horse. While a certain amount of physical strength is called for, good muscle control and responsiveness over the whole body is more important in enabling you to control a bolting horse than strong arms. Riding can be tiring because of the physical demands made on the rider and, therefore, the fitter you are the more likely you are to be able to enjoy it.

Flexibility, too, is important as a good rider needs to be able to move and change position quickly and easily. The basic process of mounting and dismounting is a good example, as you need to be very supple in your limbs and your back to be able to make the necessary movements. A horse's gaits can be very jarring on the body and to minimize this it is important to be flexible enough to follow the movements of the horse.

TIP

If riding on a different saddle, first adjust the stirrup leathers from the ground. A useful rule of thumb is to place your fingertips at the top of the leathers and stretch them along the length of your arm to a point just before your armpit. This is not an infallible method as the proportions of individuals' legs and arms vary considerably, but at least when mounted your stirrup adjustments should be minimal.

Good balance is an essential. The nature of a horse's movements require you constantly to change your centre of gravity. You need to be able to do this instinctively so that you can concentrate on directing and controlling the horse. An unbalanced rider can never be in a position of control. Balance on a horse can be greatly improved with practice. The more riding you do, the more your body will become accustomed to the different kinds of movement a horse makes and learn to cope naturally with them.

Perhaps the most important ingredient to achieving a good standard of riding ability is attitude. To be a good rider you have to want to ride and to have a fondness, if not outright love, for horses. Horses are very instinctive animals and will respond quickly to signs of tension or fear in their riders. They may respond by becoming tense themselves or simply taking advantage of the situation to misbehave. Riding is not a matter of rider dominating horse – it is a partnership where each must trust the other. If you

have a positive attitude, mingled with affection for what are undeniably beautiful creatures, you will enjoy riding more, as either sport or recreation, and are more likely to be successful.

THE BASICS

The ability to ride begins with your position in the saddle, commonly referred to as one's seat. A good seat is one where you have maximum body contact with the saddle, which allows you to remain as close as possible to the horse, and the correct positioning of back, arms and legs to maintain balance.

Not surprisingly, some people find sitting astride a horse, 1.5 m (4 ft 6 in) off the ground with no back support and nothing to hold on to, an unnatural and uncomfortable experience. Practice and familiarization are the key. You need to become accustomed to the feel of sitting in a saddle in the correct position so it begins to come naturally. The correct position is also the most

ABOVE: *Riding on a lunge line with no reins helps to improve a rider's balance*

comfortable, so if after some practice you still feel uncomfortable or unbalanced you need to review your position. Equally important is to remain relaxed. A body which is tense tends to adopt awkward postures whereas a good seat encourages a relaxed body in control of itself.

The basics of a good seat are first, to position yourself squarely in the middle of the saddle between pommel and cantle, and with a line from the horse's neck through the middle of your body so that your weight is evenly distributed on either side of the horse. Second, straighten your back and head so that that they are comfortably aligned, shoulders back and your eyes looking between the horse's ears. Do not stiffen your back or arch it. Pulling in your stomach muscles should help you find the right angle.

Third, relax your shoulders and let your arms between shoulder and elbow hang naturally at your sides. Many riders tend to use their arms for balance and stick out their elbows in a 'flying' position, which is both unattractive and actually makes the rider more unbalanced.

Fourth, position your hands either side of the horse's neck so that your forearms are angled slightly inwards. The hands should always be kept low – no more than a few centimetres off the horse's neck. Raising your hands tends to make the horse raise his head. The ideal is to keep a horse's nose and head down so you have better control.

The position of the legs is perhaps most important as it is these which anchor you to your mount and give you the most body contact with the horse. The length of your stirrups will affect the angle and contact of your leg with the horse so it is important that the stirrup length be adjusted to the rider and not vice versa. Begin to find the correct position by letting your legs hang down loosely by the horse's sides, dangling your feet. Next, raise your toes so that they are level with or slightly higher than your heels.

Finally, keeping the lower leg in position, raise your thighs up the horse so that you can grip the saddle with both the insides of your knees and thighs. This is the basis of a good seat and also gives you the correct position for the stirrups. With feet in stirrups, your lower leg should be angled towards the back of the horse, but not so far as to encourage you to point your toes downwards.

Overall, when viewed from the side, the rider should be erect but not arched, head up, with his heels roughly on a line with his shoulders. When viewed from the back, the toes should be

ABOVE: *Dressage is the ultimate test of horse and rider control.*

pointing straight – not angled out – knees in, elbows in, and body placed squarely in the middle of the horse. Unfortunately for the rider, it is not possible to see their position in the saddle and this is where professional or experienced advice is valuable. It is all too easy to become accustomed to an incorrect posture or leg position which you will need to unlearn, so help in the early stages is important.

AIDS AND CONTROL

The reins are not the only means of controlling or directing a horse. A rider has many more useful aids, and provided these are well learned by both horse and rider, they can be considerably more effective. The use of voice, legs, heels, shifting of the rider's weight and a 'good pair of hands' can, in many cases, eliminate the need for a riding crop or martingale, and are a better alternative to finding yourself in the position of standing in your stirrups, pulling with all your might to rein in a galloping horse.

Some horses need encouragement, some need control. All horses will need both at some stage. The basics of encouragement are quite simple; control requires greater experience and a 'feel' for the horse.

When encouraging a horse to move on, slow down, or make a transition into another gait, it is important to maintain a good 'contact' with its mouth via the reins. Pressure from legs and thighs combined with a firm tone of voice is a more positive

ABOVE: *The correct riding position for hands and legs.*

RIGHT: *The correct leg position gives the rider balanced control.*

signal for a horse to move forward or accelerate. Some horses require more than this. In these cases the principle should be to progress from the least severe method onwards. The next step is a gentle tapping against the horse's flanks with your heels. If this fails try a firm kick. A sharp tap with a riding crop should finally produce results. If not, ask someone to lead the horse on.

Horses sometimes need encouragement when facing unfamiliar obstacles or situations. In these cases it is essential for the rider to relax, let the horse have a look at whatever frightens them, and with reins quite loose, angle the body forward, squeeze with the legs and tap with the heels at the horse's flanks. In a jumping situation where the horse is about to refuse, a very firm squeeze with the legs and a shout should put him over. However, before you push him on you need to make a judgement about whether he is balking at something ordinary or at a potentially dangerous situation.

Control of a horse is the ability to get him to follow your directions. The most difficult situations which arise are where a horse has become too excitable or frightened to follow

commands. In these cases the rider must attempt to calm the horse and restore his confidence. This is best done by making sure you have a firm seat and are in a balanced position, as an unbalanced rider will merely add to a horse's confusion. Speak gently and soothingly to him, at the same time rein back in stages rather than hard and constantly. The idea is to get the horse to gradually collect himself rather than attempt to bring him to a complete halt. When reining in, concentrate on pulling from your stomach – rather than using your upper arms – as this will give a more controlled pressure which is better than a jerk or heavy pulling motion which could make him panic.

With an excitable horse, the best method is to get to know him well and anticipate difficult situations which you can recognize by additional pressure on the bit, a quickening or unevenness of gait, or increased tension in the horse's body beneath you.

Most horses are highly responsive, and provided the rider is aware of how to use his aids properly and is in tune with the character of the horse, control should never be a major problem between horse and rider.

MOUNTING AND DISMOUNTING

The process of mounting is a good test of both a rider's flexibility and a horse's manners. Not all horses enjoy the shift of weight involved in mounting and it is not uncommon for them to refuse to stand still. It is, therefore, important that a rider mounts as quickly and smoothly as possible.

Always mount from the horse's near, or left, side. Take the reins evenly in your left hand so that you have light contact with his mouth, and grasp the pommel of the saddle. Facing towards the horse's tail, take the stirrup iron in your right hand and turn it clockwise towards you so it is parallel to the horse's body. Insert your left foot. Using your left foot as a pivot point, pull your body up, swing your right leg over the horse's rump and down the other side, while maintaining your balance over the middle of the horse with the left hand. Find your right stirrup with your right foot, avoiding poking the horse with your toe, and slide your foot in.

LEFT: *Mount from the left-hand side of the horse, placing your left foot in the stirrup.*
BELOW LEFT: *Pull your body up using the left foot as a pivot.*
BELOW: *Swing your right leg clear over the horse's rump.*

Dismounting should also be performed as a smooth and continuous action. Hold the reins in your left hand and remove both feet from the stirrups. Using your right hand on the pommel of the saddle for balance, lean slightly forward and swing your right leg over the horse's rump and down the other side to meet your left leg and slide down the horse's side. As you swing your leg over the horse, your body will move naturally from a forward

ABOVE : *Exercising on the lunge teaches the horse to carry its head at the correct angle and the rider how to maintain a good seat.*

to a sideways position. At this point you should lean over the saddle towards the horse's right side in order to counterbalance the weight of your legs. Land lightly on both feet, facing the saddle and keeping light contact with the reins.

HOW TO:

WALK

From a standing start, move your hands slightly forward easing off on the reins and squeezing the horse's sides with both legs. If the horse refuses to move, try making a clicking noise with your tongue, or touch the horse's side firmly with your feet.

TROT

Take up the reins slightly and squeeze gently with the legs to alert the horse. Squeeze more firmly and move your hands forward to give the horse his head while encouraging him forward with your body.

CANTER

From a walk, collect the horse by tightening reins and squeezing gently, preparing him for a change of pace. Move the lower half of your outside leg slightly behind the girth, your inside leg onto the girth and shift your weight to the lead side very slightly. If your horse is attentive he will make the transition smoothly.

From a trot, sit to the trot for a few strides then turn the horse's head, lean and apply leg pressure as above.

HALT/CHANGE TO A SLOWER GAIT

Straighten your body with shoulders slightly back and shift your weight towards the horse's hindquarters, relaxing your legs. Ease back gently on the reins, applying intermittent pressure and then releasing. Do not pull suddenly or attempt to hold the horse back in one single movement.

BACK

Let the horse relax so his head is held evenly or slightly dropped. Sit well back on the horse keeping hands low and legs relaxed. Give a series of short gentle tugs on the reins, releasing the pressure on the reins between tugs.

THE BASIC GAITS

All horses have four basic gaits – walk, trot, canter and gallop. For each of these the rider needs to adopt a slightly different position on the horse in terms of weight distribution, legs, seat and hands. To move between these gaits, the horse will expect certain cues which the rider must learn.

WALK

Walking is the least interesting of a horse's gaits but nevertheless provides the ideal opportunity for horse and rider to 'get the feel' of one another. For a new rider, walking allows them to practice the correct seat and hand positions and to experiment with the use of the various aids. It is also the most comfortable and relaxing of a horse's movements and good for generating confidence in both horse and rider.

A good time to test the horse's responsiveness and your skill at handling him is at a walk. Try making him turn, halt and back up as well as walking slowly or at an extended walk.

TROT

The trot is a bouncy two-beat pace which, depending on the individual horse, can be very jarring. Most riders therefore rise in the saddle to the trot, which is known as posting or rising trot.

Posting consists of an up-down motion of the rider's seat in time to the horse's two-beat gait. It can take some time to master this rhythm, and practice is the only answer. When posting, incline the upper body slightly forward but without hunching your shoulders. On the first beat, let the action of the horse throw your seat up and forward. On the second beat allow your seat to return to the saddle, ready for the next upward movement. Your weight should be taken evenly along the leg. Do not attempt to raise yourself from the knees or use the stirrups, but let your body move naturally with the horse. Some riders tend to pull themselves up from the reins. This will tend to confuse the horse and is a misuse of the horse's mouth.

CANTER

The canter is probably the most enjoyable gait. It consists of a three-beat rolling motion to which the rider generally sits.

At a canter the horse will lead with one or other of his forelegs. The leading leg should be the one which is nearest to the inside of the circle or angle in which the horse is travelling – the left leg when travelling to the left or in an anti-clockwise direction.

At the transition to canter the rider should lean slightly forward, but with enough weight distributed towards the rear of the horse to maintain a downward pressure of the body on the saddle. Once in canter, the ideal is to retain as much contact with the saddle as possible by rocking forwards and backwards with the motion of the horse. A shorter rein is called for at the canter so the horse remains collected and maintains an even gait. Some horses have a tendency to buck at a canter and so it is important outside the schooling arena to keep the horse's head up – this also allows him a good view of where he is going which can be important over rough ground.

ABOVE: *Walking is the most comfortable of a horse's gaits.*
RIGHT: *Trotting is a rhythmic two-beat gait.*
BELOW RIGHT: *Cantering is a rolling three-beat gait.*

GALLOP

The gallop is the final and fastest gait, consisting of a rapid four-time step sequence. Galloping for a beginner would be inadvisable, because, apart from being fast and therefore dangerous, a good deal of balance is required on the rider's part. When pushing on from canter into gallop most riders find it most comfortable to ride slightly off the cantle of the saddle – in a half-posting position – gripping with thighs and lower legs. This minimizes the bouncing of seat on saddle and helps maintain balance. The rider's head should be raised, looking over the horse's ears, with the arms and hands held forward to the point where the horse can be reined in without having to shorten the grip on the reins. At this sort of speed it is imperative that you allow the horse's head movement through flexibility in your hands and arms. To slow the horse, pull back on the reins a little and slowly come back into the saddle. Once your seat is regained you will slow to a canter because horses generally find it too uncomfortable to gallop with the rider's full weight in the saddle!

IMPROVING YOUR SKILLS

ABOVE: *Jumping, showing the changing position of the rider's body.*

The process of learning never stops in horse-riding, regardless of your level of experience. Experienced riders often develop bad habits or idiosyncrasies over time of which they are not aware, and so periodic lessons are a good idea to check your style, form and technique.

For the novice, mastering the basic gaits is only the beginning. There are numerous further exercises to challenge you and improve your seat and balance. The practice of riding without stirrups will improve leg control. Balance can be increased by riding bareback or on a lunge line without reins. However, do not attempt these until you are sure you are really ready, and have the benefit of experienced or professional supervision. Another good test of both horse and rider is to try figures of eight at the trot and canter.

For all riders, one of the most valuable experiences is to ride as many different horses of different types as possible. A good rider should be able to ride almost any horse – not just their own. A

strange horse can teach you a world of new things, not only about how differently horses can perform, but also about your own performance.

LEARNING TO JUMP

The process of learning to jump should be a gradual one for both horse and rider. For the rider it should not be attempted until a very good standard of balance, control and confidence has been achieved.

The first step is typically to practice walking and then trotting over a series of poles laid on the ground at intervals corresponding to the horse or pony's stride. When riding over these the rider should lean slightly forward and advance his hands, allowing the horse to dip his head slightly to get a clearer view of the obstacles.

A worthwhile second step is trotting over cavalletti. These are a series of low poles which can be varied in height, supported by a

low X-frame. This accustoms the rider to greater 'bounce' in the horse's gait and improves balance.

When learning to jump it is best to start over simple rails set at a low level. The height will depend on the size of horse or pony but should probably not exceed 45–60 cm (18–24 in) for a medium-sized horse. Start from a trot at first, then try cantering.

When approaching a fence it is important to keep the horse's head and body straight, at a right-angle to the jump. The rider's weight should be shifted forward and the upper body inclined. At the point of take-off, the rider should lean forward in the saddle so the seat is slightly off the saddle, legs set behind the girth and gripping firmly with legs and knees. The horse's head and neck will extend naturally as it takes the jump and therefore you need to allow him enough rein by moving your hands and arms forward.

On landing, the rider should shift his or her weight back on to the saddle to help the horse recover his balance. It is essential for the rider to stay in balance at this stage and not pull on the reins to steady himself or fall forward on the horse's neck. Any reining in should be done only after all four of the horse's feet have touched the ground.

ABOVE: *Trotting over low poles teaches the horse how to approach a jump.*

BELOW: *Learning to jump can begin on the leading-rein.*

Once you have mastered the timing and balance required for jumping a single fence, you should practice jumping over several fences in succession, at varying distances so you learn to judge the number of strides the horse needs to take between obstacles. Also experiment with different types of fences, gradually increasing the height and width. These call for slightly different timing and techniques. As in most things, experience is the best teacher, but professional guidance can be invaluable.

FALLING AND INJURY

No rider, however experienced, is immune from falling or some kind of injury. The best way to avoid both is to be prepared.

The experience of a fall can bruise confidence, pride, body – or all three. The old adage about re-mounting straightaway has much to recommend it. Falling should not be regarded as exceptional, but part of the normal learning process. The best way to prevent a bad experience from turning into hardened fear or embarrassment is to deal with it at the time. This is true for both horse and rider. However, the immediate remedy will depend on individual circumstances and may require support from those around. All riders need to be aware of the need to be calm, and to restore confidence after a fall – whether you are helping or receiving help.

LEFT: *If you relax when you fall only your pride should be hurt.*

With a very few exceptions, horses are not inherently dangerous or malicious animals. The major proportion of accidents or injuries are the result of carelessness or ignorance on the part of riders or handlers. Even the most familiar and quiet horse can sometimes behave in unpredictable ways and you should never take a horse's behaviour for granted. This does not mean you should mistrust them, but rather do not take risks – for example, walking closely behind a horse, or riding on such a loose rein that you cannot possibly recover control. 'Daredevil' practices such as racing over unfamiliar ground or putting your horse at speed to obstacles which are unfamiliar or too demanding, only shows a rider's preparedness to risk his horse – and himself. This is not bravery, but foolishness.

Some falls and injuries cannot be avoided. However, as long as you are aware and prepared, like most experienced riders, the most you are likely to suffer is a horse standing on your foot.

BELOW: *Confidence in jumping comes with practice.*

TRAINING THE HORSE

All horses require different amounts and kinds of training depending on their age and their history. During the course of its life, a horse will usually have had several different owners – each with his own style of riding, level of experience and approach to keeping and caring for it. A horse may also have been used for many different purposes – hacking over country, indoor riding or jumping at local shows. Depending on the horse and the purpose for which you want to use it, training can mean anything from correcting bad habits to teaching a horse entirely new skills.

At its most basic, training is a matter of ensuring that a horse is fit, well-mannered, understands its cues and is reliable. Some types of training, such as breaking-in a young horse or preparing a horse for eventing, are highly specialized and require considerable expertise, if not professional help. Written guides such as this are no substitute for years of experience.

Most training, however, is actually done at a day-to-day level. Every time you ride your horse it gains more experience – of you and of its surroundings. The important thing to remember is that a horse is capable of learning bad habits as well as good, and to prevent them from learning these is as important a form of training as teaching them to jump.

FITNESS

A horse's level of fitness will depend on the amount and type of exercise it is given. This is an important aspect of training which is often overlooked. A fit horse will be much less prone to injury, and will give a more enjoyable ride.

Different breeds and types of horse require different amounts and kinds of exercise to keep them fit and happy. Thoroughbreds, for example, need considerably more work as a rule than most other breeds. However, there is no set standard, and you will need to experiment with the amount of exercise which is right for your

DAILY ROUTINES

The ideal daily routine for each horse will depend on the level of exercise it needs, and on how it is used. However, there are a few general points which apply to most horses which you should consider in planning your regular workouts.

FIRST, provided your horse is in a reasonable state of fitness, it should be ridden at all three gaits, with a balance between the time spent on each. Horses need the discipline and the particular type of exercise they get from all three gaits, and it is a mistake to ignore walking and trotting for the sake of the more comfortable and exciting ride you get from cantering.

SECOND, horses, like left- and right-handed people, often prefer circling in one direction, or favour a certain lead at canter. The basic aim should be to have a horse who is as balanced as possible regardless of his direction or lead.

THIRD, when working your horse, do not repeat the same routine each time you ride. There are many different variations which you can introduce to prevent a horse from becoming bored or inattentive.

FOURTH, try and expose your horse to as many different environments and types of terrain as possible to widen his experience and extend his confidence.

Finally, general riding should be complemented by a regular period of training or schooling – either for a few minutes a day if you are attempting to teach the horse a new skill, or once or twice a week if he needs to improve on some minor point of behaviour.

ABOVE: *Even the fastest racehorses begin exercise with a loosening walk.*

horse. Bad stable behaviour is sometimes an indication that a horse is bored or has had insufficient exercise. It is a good idea when buying a horse to ask the previous owner how much and what type of work the horse is accustomed to.

As with any physical exercise, whether in humans or horses, it is best to start slowly and gradually work up to the standard of performance you hope to achieve. In a very unfit horse this can mean a lot of walking initially so the horse builds up muscle tone and stamina. Gradually, trotting can be added to the routine, and in the later stages, a combination of the first three gaits will give the horse a balanced workout. The occasional gallop is also a very important part of the exercise routine, once a horse has reached a good state of fitness.

As a general rule, start slowly when exercising your horse and allow the muscles to warm up. Taking a horse from the stable immediately into a canter is an invitation to leg strain. Take your time. It is also important to realize that a lot of slow work is much more beneficial to a horse than a short period of hard riding.

Horses need to be worked regularly. It is of no benefit to allow a horse to stand for several days and then work him for a long period to make up for the exercise he has missed. Horses do also need rest, particularly after a hard day's showing or riding out. If the horse is stabled, it is a good idea the following day to simply lead him out on a lead rein to stretch his muscles and let him relax in the open air. Alternatively, you could turn him out in a paddock for the day to release any pent-up tension.

VARIETY

A common mistake in training a horse is to repeat the same daily routine in the same place. While horses like a consistent regime in their general care, they need variety in their working routine to bring out the best in them. Some horses do not actually mind doing the same thing day after day as it does not challenge or stretch them. Others become bored and can begin to misbehave. For a horse to reach his full potential, it is important that he has as many different kinds of experience as possible.

An easy change to make is to vary the sequence in which he does his gaits. Make sure that you do not always start out in the same direction. For example, walk the horse in both directions for enough time to get his muscles warmed, then try cantering him at a very collected pace. Turn him in the other direction, walk for a bit, then trot. From the trot go into a canter. Come back to a walk, turn and then trot in the other direction. This change of routine improves a horse's concentration and makes sure that he recognizes the rider's signal for different gaits, regardless of whether they are in sequence.

Another useful change of routine is to practise figures of eight or changes of direction. Figures of eight can be done at walk, trot and canter. The horse should remain balanced, turning gradually, rather than 'leaning' or holding its head to one side. Simple changes of direction at the trot and canter are good for maintaining a horse's attention and improving balance.

A good alternative to riding is lunging. This is typically used for young horses to accustom them to the bit and being saddled. For a more experienced horse this can be a useful change of routine and a good oportunity for training the carriage of the horse's head. Lunging involves working the horse in a circle, without rider, on a long line around his trainer. There are various different types of lunge tackle, each with different bitting arrangements. The most common are either a ring attached to the cavesson with no bit, or side reins which are connected to a roller on the girth which control the angle of the horse's head.

Horses respond differently in different physical surroundings. Ideally, you never want to be in a position where your horse misbehaves or under-performs because his concentration is

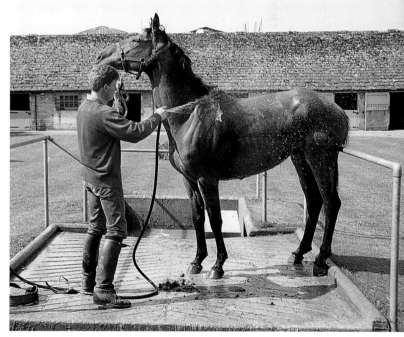

ABOVE: *After heavy exercise the horse may need to be washed down before grooming.*

ABOVE: *Horses cantering in the Camargue, France.*

FIGURES OF EIGHT (OPPOSITE)

★ Begin by making your circles quite large and gradually tighten them as the horse becomes more accustomed to the movement.
★ At a trot, once you have completed the first loop of your figure, continue through the centre without stopping and make a circle in the opposite direction. As you cross the centre point, bounce once so that you are posting on the correct diagonal i.e. sitting as the horse's inside front leg moves forward.
★ At a canter, the horse should change leads as he reaches the centre point and changes direction. This can take some time to learn, and it may be helpful at first to slow to a trot in the centre and then make the transition to canter on the correct lead.

totally distracted by new circumstances, or he feels insecure about the ground or general environment. Clearly, you cannot plan for every situation, but it is important for the horse's confidence – and your own – to subject him to as much variety as possible.

Every horse should have some experience of being ridden in different situations – in open country, on roads and in some kind of enclosure – preferably both covered and open-air. Horses used to being ridden in an enclosure may be difficult to control in open spaces. If you are riding outside an enclosure for the first time, it is a good idea, if possible, to take a companion on a more experienced horse. This should give the novice horse confidence, and means that in case of problems you will have help on hand.

Riding out on roads and bridleways is also good experience and provides the horse with different kinds of stimulation. Some horses panic at the sound of their own hooves on tarmac, while others are afraid of cars. On a bridleway there are many unusual shapes, sounds and movement which may frighten some horses. The only remedy for fear is familiarity. Expose them gradually and more frequently to what they fear and be patient with them.

Again, another horse may help give confidence.

A horse also needs variety in the terrain over which it is worked, for both experience and muscle building. A reliable horse is one who knows where to place his feet and how to keep his balance over uneven ground and up and down slopes. This ability is particularly important when moving at speed. An inexperienced mount can be quite dangerous, as many horses tend to panic and travel faster without any regard to their footing or what lies ahead. Try your horse in as many different types of situation as possible, and try to think ahead and anticipate problems before they occur.

Slopes and uneven ground are an ideal addition to any working routine as they exercise not only a horse's shoulders, hindquarters, back and neck, but also his eye coordination and overall balance.

BELOW: *Lunging prior to competition keeps the horse relaxed and warmed up.*

FIGURE OF EIGHT

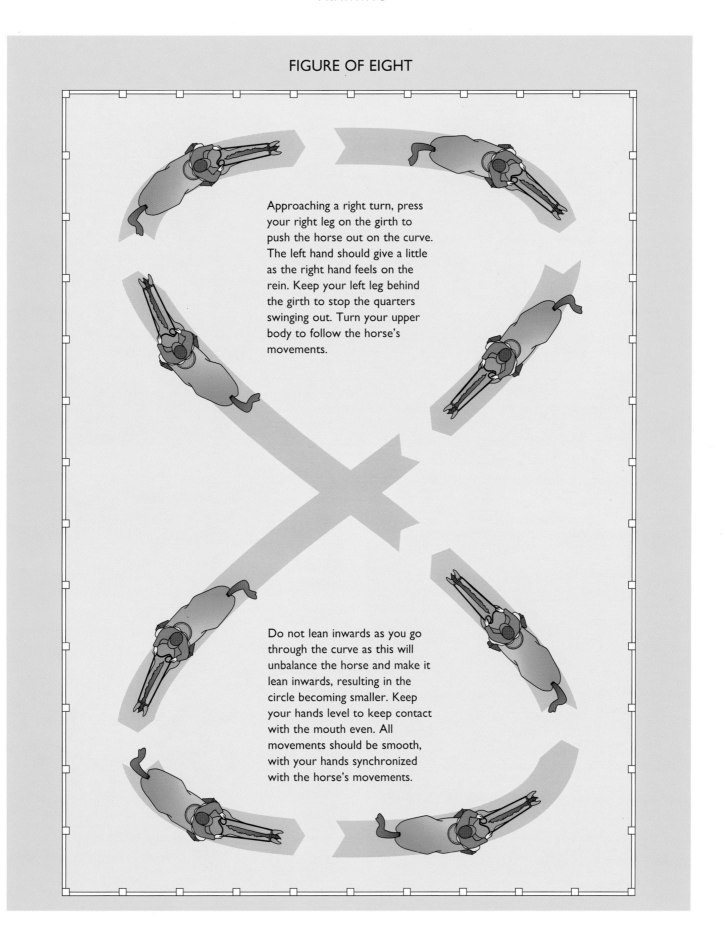

Approaching a right turn, press your right leg on the girth to push the horse out on the curve. The left hand should give a little as the right hand feels on the rein. Keep your left leg behind the girth to stop the quarters swinging out. Turn your upper body to follow the horse's movements.

Do not lean inwards as you go through the curve as this will unbalance the horse and make it lean inwards, resulting in the circle becoming smaller. Keep your hands level to keep contact with the mouth even. All movements should be smooth, with your hands synchronized with the horse's movements.

ABOVE: *Well-mannered ponies with well-mannered riders.*

BELOW: *A well-schooled horse will always help the rider to learn.*

GOOD MANNERS

Whatever the standard or ability of a horse, above all else it should be trained to observe good manners both in the stable and when riding out.

At walk, the horse should keep a steady pace, not slowing down or speeding up suddenly. It is also important to be able to keep to a 'flat' walk, without prancing or jogging about. This is particularly important when slowing from trot or canter. If your horse has difficulty maintaining a constant pace, make sure that he is well-collected by squeezing gently with your legs at the same time as keeping him slightly reined in and off the bit. For horses which have difficulty settling to a walk, the rider should shift his weight slightly further back in the saddle while reining in a little at a time. A comforting pat on the horse's neck may also help to settle him.

At trot, the horse should maintain an even rhythm without the need for undue pressure on the bit. The horse should carry his head up and nose down with neck flexed – not extended straight out as this encourages a 'shuffling' trot. Some horses have a tendency to break into a canter. In such cases, an occasional nudge back on the bit when you feel the horse start to change pace should keep him in a trot. Do not, however, attempt to hold the horse back by constant pressure on the bit as he is more likely to pull against you and become even more unsettled. The transition from a walk to a trot should be very smooth with the horse cued by leg pressure and hand control, without the need for kicking the horse or use of a riding crop.

When cantering, the horse should remain collected and not pull on the bit or attempt to race. The head should be held level, with the nose pointing downwards slightly more than at a trot, in order to increase the rider's control. Ideally, horses which become very excitable at a canter should be worked in enclosed spaces or in fairly tight circles until they become accustomed to cantering at a controlled pace. A horse should be trained to move to canter from either walk or trot, and not have to be run into canter by progressively faster and faster trotting. The cue for a particular lead should involve only a slight shift in the rider's weight and leg pressure on the lead side, and enough pressure on the reins to maintain a good contact with the horse's mouth to prevent it from running on.

The ability to halt, stand still, and back on command is a sign of a well-schooled horse. This indicates not only that the horse is sensitive to the bit but also that he is attentive to the rider and under control. Many horses find it difficult to stand still, particularly when asked to come to a halt from a fast trot or canter. This is partly a matter of practice so the horse understands what is expected of him, but may also call for calming tactics such as shifting weight to the back of the saddle, a soothing voice and a reassuring pat.

BAD HABITS

There are a number of bad habits which horses can acquire which cannot be rectified in the course of simple regular training. These demand specific measures to deal with them, which any rider or owner should know and should implement – with or without experienced help.

BUCKING

Some horses buck as a demonstration of high spirits, often as a result of insufficient exercise. For others, it is a bad habit to be tried at any opportunity, particularly at the canter and gallop. The best way of dealing with a horse that bucks is to keep it on a sufficiently tight rein so that it cannot lower its head and therefore cannot raise its hindquarters. Persistent attempts at

ABOVE: *Riding lessons are aimed at teaching the correct body position for all four gaits.*

bucking should be punished either by using your heels or a riding crop, but you will need to keep a tight seat. There is one other possibility for persistent bucking: a horse might have a bad back making it painful for it to carry a rider's weight. If you suspect this is the case, ask an experienced horseman to have a look, it might save you and your horse much heartache and bruises.

REARING

Horses usually rear only in exceptional circumstances, though there are some for whom this is an habitual bad practice. If a horse rears, on no account pull on the reins as this will tend to off-balance the horse and may pull him over. Instead, give the

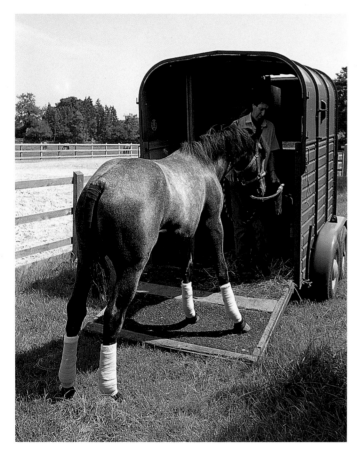

LEFT: *Biting horses need to be treated firmly.*
BELOW LEFT: *Boxing a horse can take time and patience.*
BELOW: *Rearing is a horse's natural way of fighting.*

horse his head by putting your hands forward, steadying yourself on his neck for balance if necessary. For horses who rear frequently, a hand placed on the crest of the horse's neck will encourage him to keep his head down. A firm tap between the ears is also a useful disincentive.

BOXING

Difficulties in boxing are quite common and while they are typically the result of fear rather than a malicious nature, can be very dangerous to horse and handlers. The critical point is to allow sufficient time. Do not, under any circumstances, rush the horse, because this will only increase his anxiety. If you know your horse has a problem, practise beforehand if possible. Let the horse have a good look at the horse box. If he pulls away, do not resist but gradually lead him in for a closer look. Encourage him to get close and perhaps even take a step up the gangway with a bucket of feed. As a last resort, pressure from behind will usually achieve the desired result. This can be done by drawing a rope around the horse's hindquarters and up each side, or more simply by two people locking hands around the horse's tail and guiding him on either side with their free arms.

BITING

Some horses have a tendency to bite, particularly when a rider or attendant's attention is distracted. This is not generally a habit which can be cured by kindness, though if the horse attempts to bite only on specific occasions you should investigate whether this is a sign that he is in pain or that something is troubling him. If you are satisfied that this is not the case, a shout or ultimately a sound smack should be used to alert him to the fact that this is not tolerable behaviour.

KICKING

Kicking can either be something a horse does in specific circumstances, or a general habit involving people or horses. This is a potentially very dangerous habit and one which you can acquire unknowingly with a new horse. Some horses kick in their stables because of a lack of exercise. Horses also kick because they do not like what is happening to them – such as being shod or having their tails washed. This should be regarded as exceptional, but nevertheless a horse who tends to kick as a protest should never be regarded as safe.

If you know a horse tends to kick at specific times, take the precaution of putting a bridle on it so you can be in a greater position of control and also distract its attention. Horses who kick unexpectedly or during normal handling are usually very highly strung. The best you can do is make sure the horse is approached slowly and calmly in every aspect of care – and keep a wide berth!

ABOVE: *If a horse rears do not pull on the reins.*
BELOW: *Preparing horses ready to box.*

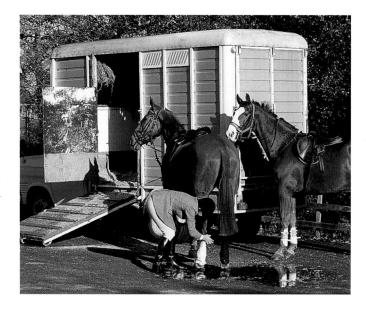

Chapter 5
SHOWING AND COMPETING

For some the excitement that showing and competition generates is their major

reason for their involvement with horses, while for others it is a chance to meet new people

who also love this most noble of animals. Because there is a lot of waiting between classes

you cannot help getting to know your fellow competitors, and this might turn out

to be one of the lasting benefits of attending such events. Certainly many people have made

great friends out of riding as everyone tends to go to the same shows, entering the same classes,

week after week, especially during summer.

SHOWS AND GYMKHANAS

Your local Pony Club or Riding Club branch will probably organize regular shows throughout summer. There is usually a wide variety of events and they are graded so that there is something for everyone, whatever the size or breed of the horse or pony or the age and skill of the rider. To enter you will have to join the club for a small fee and you will then receive schedules of the events so that you can choose which competitions you wish to enter. The rules of the club will be printed on the inside of the schedule and you should read these carefully – riding crops and spurs might be banned, for example. It is sensible to put in your entry before the event – first because it allows you the time to organize yourself, second it helps the show organizers to run things smoothly, and third there is usually a reduction in the entry fee.

LEFT: *King Boris and Mary Thomson in the water at Burghley.*

For children under seven years there are leading-rein classes for ponies under 12 hands where the child is mounted but lead by and assistant – usually a long-suffering parent – who can also help to untack the horse if it is required. Leading-rein jumping over 'minimus' brush fences might also be included, and tests the fitness of the assistant as much as the pony. Remember, these classes are meant to be a fun introduction to competition.

Leading-rein classes are a great introduction to shows and allow a young rider to feel confident in a competitive situation. Everyone is there to encourage the young rider to continue through the ranks to the more senior classes.

For the more advanced rider there are a variety of classes including events such as the Handy Pony class where the pony and rider will be asked to pass through an equine obstacle course and complete tasks such as opening a gate, backing up or removing a bag from a line against time.

RIDING OUT

When the time comes to leave the comfort of the home field or menage, you should be confident, in control of your horse and able to deal with any situation. It is also useful to practise opening and closing gates while mounted. The important rules of riding out are to keep safety paramount in your mind and show consideration for other users of the countryside. Follow the Country Code and all traffic regulations as they apply as much to horse and rider as any other person.

While on the road, keep the horses in single file so cars have plenty of room to pass. Always slow the horse to a walk when cars want to pass and, as most cars will slow and give you a wide berth, it is only polite to thank them by tipping your hat or raising your riding crop and smiling. In autumn and winter, when dusk comes early, wear something that shows up in the dark. Luminous bibs, sashes and armbands reflect light on dark clothing. Special lights are available that can be strapped to the rider's ankle or attached to the stirrup irons – the natural movement of the legs gives a good warning signal. If possible, take a Road Safety course when it is offered by one of the local Pony Clubs. They also offer First Aid courses by qualified first-aiders because it is important to know what to do if there is a riding accident.

Always keep to official bridleways and riding tracks and never trespass on private property. Most farmers are happy to allow responsible riders to use the field tracks if asked, but do not ride through any crops or frighten other animals. All gates must be closed after you have passed through them and never ride at speed past people walking. This is not just courtesy, it might frighten the walkers and in turn scare your horse.

Most shows end with the gymkhana, which is a series of mounted races and games. These are great fun for spectators and participants alike (including the ponies!), and often give young riders their first taste of heated competition. Rosettes are awarded down to sixth place in most classes, and there is sometimes a trophy for the winner.

SHOW CLOTHING

Horse shows are rather traditional in their attitude to riders' dress, and in showing classes the state of a rider's clothing may well decide the eventual winner in the judge's eyes. Hats must fit properly, be clean and the nap flat – steaming them with a kettle and smoothing works well. The hat and jacket must also match and many colours are available for the show ring – navy blue, green, brown or grey. For the working hunter classes, stick to navy blue or tweed. When choosing a colour try to make it complement the colour of the coat of the horse.

Jodhpurs should be traditional white, beige, cream or lemon, rather than a jazzy colour. Jodhpur boots can be black or brown, but consideration should be given to the colour of the tack, which itself should be chosen to complement the horse's colouring.

ABOVE: *Gymkhana mounted games are a feature of most horse shows.*

LEFT: *Pony trekking on Exmoor.*

RIGHT: *Waiting to jump at a Pony Club show.*

PLAITING

Plaiting the mane, tail and forelock gives the horse or pony a neat appearance and is expected in most showing and jumping classes. It is best done on the day of the show, rather than the night before, and can be done at the show ground. Skills in plaiting increase with practice, but you only really need the correct equipment, patience and an eye for detail. In showing classes of native breeds the mare should not be plaited, and if jumping later the pony will need to be plaited at the show.

MANE PLAITING

First, divide the mane up into even bunches and hold each bunch together with an elastic band. Traditionally a working hunter has seven plaits, plus the forelock, but for other show and ridden ponies the number does not really matter – only the appearance. Second, beginning at the poll, take off the elastic band from the first bunch of mane hair and dampen and then comb it straight. Now plait tightly from the top to the end – as far as you can go – and sew up the end with plaiting thread. Wrap the thread around the spiky end and sew it under. Finally, roll the plait under to the neck and sew it in. Any stray hairs can be trimmed off. Repeat the plaiting down the mane, ensuring that the plaits are even.

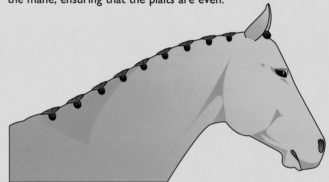

TAIL PLAITING

The tail should be washed, combed and then straightened by applying a tail bandage. The aim is to produce a French plait down to the end of the dock and then finish off with a conventional plait to the full length of the tail hair. Begin by selecting three hanks of hair about the thickness of a finger – one from each side and one from the middle of the tail. The plait leads left over right and continues in conventional fashion, regularly bringing in hanks from the edges of the tail until the end of the dock is reached. Once the normal plaiting takes over, continue until the plait is level with the bottom of the tail. Finish by securing the end with thread and sewing it back into the plait to create a loop.

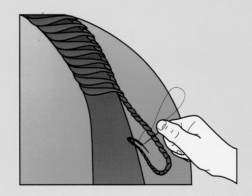
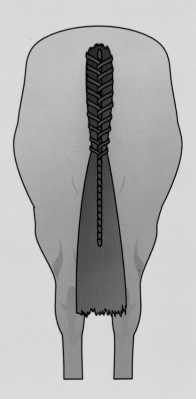

ABOVE: *A buttonhole should be worn in showing classes.*
BELOW: *Lead rein showing requires the assistant to dress as well.*

GETTING READY

Preparing for the show begins the day before. The horse should be washed with a horse shampoo and groomed during the day. If possible, stable the horse overnight to keep it clean. Alternatively, if the horse is turned out, use a New Zealand rug to keep the coat as clean as possible. In the evening, give your tack a really good clean and prepare the rider's show clothing. You will need a show hat, show jacket, jodhpurs of the appropriate colour, jodhpur boots or riding boots, a white shirt, a tie and, if you have long hair, a hair-net. A modest buttonhole should be worn in showing classes. Remember, the turn-out of the rider is as important as that of the horse.

On the morning of the show, start early enough to prepare the horse properly. A final grooming is needed: hooves should be cleaned and oiled, and the horse's mane and tail plaited as necessary – native ponies in some show classes, for example, should not be plaited. If boxed, the horse should be protected by a tail-bandage, knee and leg bandages and boots.

When you arrive at the show, register with the committee. You will receive your number which you must wear as instructed by the officials. Check the layout of the show so that you will know exactly where to go. Classes will usually be called over a tannoy system so make sure you are listening and turn up on time – if you are late then you may be disqualified.

ETIQUETTE

In showing classes all the contestants are often in the ring at the same time, but do not jostle to get in first. Keep yourself and your horse controlled and relaxed. In jumping and dressage classes, riders are called by their number and the order will usually be posted on a board at the entrance to the ring. Again, do not hurry to get in, always wait for the previous rider to leave first.

In some classes the judges may ask the rider questions, such as the age and name of the horse and the rider should be prepared to speak in a clear voice and answer with confidence. Smiling helps, too. Always be polite to the judges – they make the decisions!

After the class, the winners will be announced, perhaps from first to sixth place, and will be asked to line up in order to be presented with their rosettes and possibly a small trophy for the winner. Non-winners then leave the ring while the winners do a lap of honour.

SHOW-JUMPING FENCES

Fences are built with two elements in mind – height and width. Brush, poles, poles and brush, and walls are typical of height fences; parallel bars, triple bars and double oxers for spread, although any fence might contain a combination of both. Initially a fence might look easy, but remember the course-builder often includes hidden problems like difficult and tight lines between fences, or odd distances between elements in a double – this is why walking the course is an essential exercise.

SHOW-JUMPING

Show-jumping classes are classified by the height of the fences, by the age of the child and the height of the pony. They begin with very small brush fences and progress through different heights. As the rider progresses in ability, he or she can choose to enter whichever class desired. The usual rule, however, is that if you have won a particular class twice you cannot enter that class again, but must move up to the next. At some shows, horses and ponies may be jumped over the same course, although they are judged separately. Standard rules apply. Their are faults for a refusal, a fall and knocking down a fence. If you jump a fence out of sequence you will be disqualified. In the event of several clear rounds, there is a jump-off against the clock, usually over a reduced number of fences.

Before any jumping class begins, the order of jumps will be posted and the riders are allowed to walk the course before the event. This is the riders' opportunity to work out the correct and best route to take, to memorize the sequence of fences, the distance between them, and work out a strategy for tackling combination jumps. Watching other people's jumping rounds can also help you to decide on the best route, especially if it comes to a jump-off.

WORKING HUNTER

Working hunter classes are designed to test the temperament and abilities of both horse and rider. They consist of two stages – a showing stage, where the horse is put through its paces by the judge, and a jumping stage, which tests both riders' and horses' ability and bravery over fences. These courses are usually made to look as natural as possible, in direct contrast to the artificially constructed and coloured fences of the show-jumping ring. Some shows may include pairs and team competitions and even brother and sister or child and parent teams.

ABOVE: *Walking the course before a jumping class.*
RIGHT: *Jumping classes are organized over different height fences.*

OTHER FORMS OF COMPETITION

DRESSAGE

Dressage is a very formal form of riding and is performed to demonstrate the control of the rider and the training of the horse. Horse and rider are expected to go through their paces over a pre-selected routine, which is completed by memory. However, for beginners instructions can be given by an assistant, although this is not always permitted. Although competitors at the highest level may need to work with their horse for up to four years before they compete successfully, there are novice classes which should be treated as fun and part of the learning process. Dressage competitions are always graded according to ability and riders of similar standards compete against one another.

EVENTING

Eventing is the combination of the three main competitive disciplines: dressage, cross-country and show-jumping. At Olympic and national level these competitions take place over three days, one day being given to each discipline, while at a local level they usually take place over a single day. Eventing is a stern test of ability, fitness, stamina, athleticism and resolve for both horse and rider.

Local shows are a good way of getting to know other riders and horses in your area, but they will only take you to a certain level of competitiveness. If you want to compete at a higher level, travelling, time and costs will increase proportionately. And winning a local show does not necessarily mean you will come anywhere near winning when the competition is fierce. Only ever do what you are confident about and find fun, and remember that many great show-jumpers and eventers began on the leading rein.

ABOVE: *A cross-country rider at a Badminton three-day event.*

LEFT: *A young runner carrying the results of a cross-country race back to the judges.*

RIGHT: *Dutch Bid being ridden by Jenny Lorriston-Clarke in the dressage ring.*

Chapter 6
YOUR HORSE'S HEALTH

Horses can become ill, often with fatal consequences. As an owner your responsibility

is to recognize the signs of illness as early as possible and take the necessary action.

For the inexperienced owner the rule should always be to call your veterinarian if you

think there is a problem. Some illnesses, if not treated early, can lead to great

distress to the horse and subsequently the owner. It does help, however, if you learn

to recognize and describe the symptoms to the veterinarian as it will help him

in his diagnosis. After all, you know your horse best.

To recognize when a horse is unwell it is important to know the signs of a healthy horse, both physically and behaviourally. A healthy horse is bright-eyed, has a shine to its coat, stands equally on all four feet and is alert, with the ears warm to the touch at their base. A healthy horse is interested in what is going on around it. A horse that becomes listless, stands in one place for a long time or is reluctant to move, is most probably sickening. Any change in normal behaviour or feeding routine suggests that there is a problem.

Other symptoms are similar to human symptoms – running eyes and nose, sweating, diarrhoea, coughing and other breathing difficulties. Kicking and biting its sides, excessive rolling, standing or moving in an odd way and general bad temper also suggest the horse may have a health problem.

LEFT: *Arab mare and foal.*

PREVENTATIVE MEASURES

All horses should be immunized against tetanus and influenza – and receive regular booster shots. They must also be wormed every four or six weeks.

All horses suffer from worms and there is a wide variety of different infestations. Worms are parasites that live in the horse's intestines, feeding on the horse's digestive juices and so stealing the horse's food. Some also irritate the intestinal lining which makes it harder for the horse to absorb nutrients. Many worm species invade the blood vessels and migrate to other organs, causing severe and permanent damage.

The horse becomes infected by eating worm larvae in field grass, which then enter the intestines where they develop into egg-laying adults. The eggs are discharged in the horse's droppings and the breeding cycle starts again. Consequently, horses tend to

FIRST-AID KIT

All owners should have a first-aid kit stocked with everyday medicines – kept close at hand in the tack room and taken to any show or event. The kit should be regularly checked and any items used replaced immediately.

Make sure you also have a rudimentary knowledge of first-aid for both horses and riders. While it is useful to carry first-aid kits around with you, there might be times when you will have to resort to using whatever you can find around you. Cuts and bruises are the severest injuries most people see. If your horse or pony is cut and lame, dismount immediately and walk home. Once there, apply antibiotic powder to the cut, and if the injury is serious you might want to consult a professional.

At competitions, however, there are usually knowledgeable people around who will be happy to help you out or lend you any medical kit you might need. This is in addition to the facilities which any well-organized show will have provided on site. As for injuries to the rider, professional medical aid will usually be in attendance.

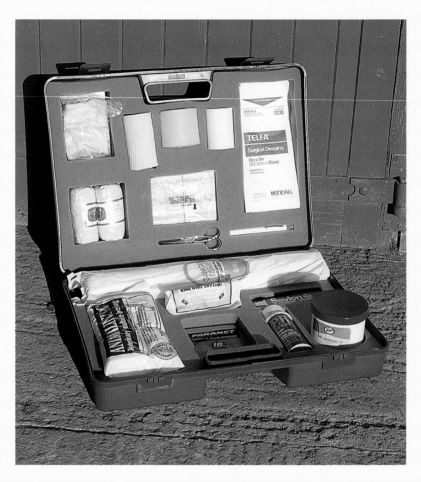

The basic travelling kit for dealing with emergencies should contain:

- 2 8-cm (3-in) crepe bandages
- 2 8-cm (3-in) rolls of sticky plaster
- 4 8-cm (3-in) gauze bandages
- Cotton wool
- Gamgee
- Packet of lint
- Paraffin gauze dressing
- Bottle of antiseptic disinfectant
- Antibiotic aerosol spray and powder puffer
- Thermometer
- Surgical scissors (with rounded ends)

In addition, a range of medicines and other equipment should be kept near at hand. These include:

- Worming powder or paste
- Poultices
- Cough medicines
- Methylated spirit
- Glycerine
- Petroleum Jelly
- Epsom and Glauber's salts
- Bandages in different sizes

TEETH

Problems with teeth can make the horse stop eating properly because chewing can be painful if teeth are sharp and overgrown, leading to loss of condition. Horses' teeth are not like human teeth – they are growing continually throughout the horse's life – and the worn surface is continually being regenerated from below. The teeth in opposite jaws wear each other down, ideally at a constant rate to keep the teeth balanced. In reality, they often wear unevenly and the sharp edges of the teeth can cut the horse's mouth and tongue. Teeth should be checked regularly and sharp edges rasped smooth by the veterinarian.

have more worms in summer when they are grazing more and will need to be wormed more regularly. If the field is used by several horses they should all be wormed at the same time. Good stable routine and good field management should help to cut down contamination.

There are many different kinds of worming drugs available so be guided by your veterinarian and follow the maker's instructions to the letter. Worm treatments come as powders that are mixed with feed or as a paste applied to the back of the tongue with a dispenser. Both of these kinds can be given by the owner, but a veterinarian will be needed to administer the forms that require a stomach tube.

Signs of worm infestation include a general poor condition with a dull coat, an extended stomach, anaemia, colic and an overall lack of performance.

SKIN DISEASES

Horses are quite susceptible to skin problems, especially in unhygenic conditions, so good stable and field management are essential.

Ringworm is a fungal infection that is contagious. It is caught from other horses, and sometimes cattle, and it can be passed on to humans. Usually it is passed from one infected horse to another through tack or grooming kit. This is one very good reason why each horse should have its own individual grooming kit.

Ringworm shows up as circular patches on the coat. These rings vary in size and may be itchy. They should be treated with

CHECKING PULSE, BREATHING AND TEMPERATURE

It is a good idea to know the normal pulse, breathing rate and temperature of your horse so that you can tell if it is feeling unwell or in pain. Individual horses vary within limits and whether they are at rest or after heavy exercise.

A normal pulse rate is somewhere between 35 and 40 per minute, but can be more than double this after being worked. The pulse can be found along the inside of the lower jaw or just behind the elbow.

A horse's normal breathing rate can vary from about 8 to 16 breaths a minute, with ponies tending to breathe faster than horses. Anything above this suggests that the horse is distressed and will probably have a temperature as well.

Take the temperature of your horse when he is fit and healthy and before exercise, and not when he is excited. It should read somewhere between 37.4°C (99.3°F) and 38.6°C (101.5°F) – anything higher suggests that the horse has a fever.

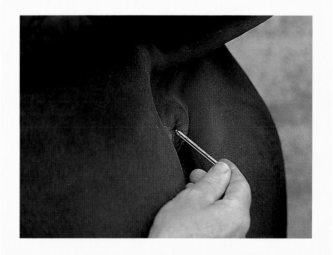

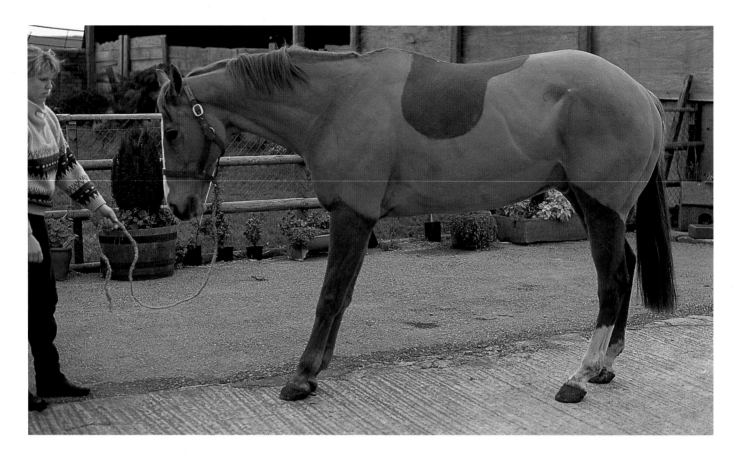

ABOVE: *Laminitis is intense inflammation of the inside wall of the foot. It can affect all four feet at the same time.*

tincture of iodine or a proprietary medicine. All tack, blankets and grooming kit must be disinfected with a recommended disinfectant – some household varieties are not effective – and the horse kept away from others until the infection has gone.

Sweet itch affects the area around the tail and mane and causes the horse to rub these areas to ease the irritation. It is an allergic reaction to the bites of certain midges which tend to attack the horse at dusk during late spring, summer and early autumn. Preventative measures include stabling the horse after four o'clock in the afternoon, using insect repellents, ensuring that there is fly-mesh on the stable windows, or using some mechanism or chemical to kill all flies in the stable area. Sweet itch can be treated by keeping the mane and tail clean and applying a soothing ointment, but consult your veterinarian.

Lice are often found on horses in winter and spring and can be passed on during grooming. They appear as small grey, black or yellow parasites in the coat which irritate the skin, making the horse scratch itself constantly, causing bald patches. Treatment is effective with a selection of de-lousing shampoos or powders, but the bald patches can take some time to grow back.

Warble fly larvae can sometimes attack horses that graze with other animals, especially cattle. The larvae migrate through the horse's legs and emerge under the skin on the horse's back creating painful swellings. The larvae can be surgically removed by the veterinarian or treated by the owner, with the veterinarian's advice, by bathing the lumps in warm water to keep them soft. The washing will draw the maggot from the small hole in the top of the lump when it can then be gently squeezed out.

Horses often develop lumps on their skin, which, if left, can turn to ulcerated sores. A common cause is badly fitting and dirty tack which rubs the horse's skin and leads to infection. Other causes may be warts, which will probably disappear without any treatment, and sarcoids, which are irregular out-growths that may need to be removed by the veterinarian using a freezing technique.

If there are any skin problems under the saddle then the horse should not be ridden until the condition improves. A numnah or pressure pad under the saddle may help the problem and should stop saddle sores from recurring.

MUD FEVER AND RAIN SCALD

Horses kept out to over-winter at grass in wet conditions are susceptible to infection from bacteria. Continually muddy legs allow bacteria to survive in the conditions they like and cause skin irritation which manifests itself by cracks in the skin that release a discharge. The legs become hot and swell. The same bacteria are responsible for rain scald on the horse's hindquarters. For the bacteria's spores to germinate, they need to be continually wet. In rainy conditions, the bacteria infect the hindquarters and develop scabs under the matted winter coat. The treatment for both conditions is to remove the scabs and expose the underlying area to the air and apply an antiseptic solution.Keep the legs dry by stabling the horse until the infection has cleared up.

CUTS, BRUISES AND SCRATCHES

A horse will pick up minor injuries, cuts and bruises for a variety of reasons – for example, scratches from shrubs or brush while grazing, cuts from sharp objects, such as unsuitable fencing, kicks or bites from another horse, broken skin on the knees if a horse trips on a hard surface and over-reach injuries where the shoes on the hind legs catch on the forelegs. The horse should be checked every day for these kinds of knocks and wounds.

Minor wounds can be treated yourself by cleaning them with warm water and cotton wool and then applying a mild disinfectant or antibiotic preparation. It is important to keep the wound clean and dry. Deep wounds may need to be stitched, a treatment which should always be left to the veterinarian. If an injury like this does occur, the wound must be kept clean with warm water or covered with gamgee cotton and a bandage until the veterinarian arrives.

Bruising from a kick or knock may result in swelling and this can be reduced by running cold water over the inflamed area.

COLIC

Colic is a severe digestive complaint which causes painful stomach-ache. It should always be regarded as an emergency and the veterinarian called immediately to give pain-killing injections and other treatment. A horse suffering from colic will keep looking at its flanks, pawing the ground and begin sweating. It may start to roll on the ground, which presents the danger of a twisted intestine – this can be fatal. While waiting for the veterinarian, keep the horse on its feet walking around and cover it with a sweat rug or blanket to keep it warm. The causes of colic are varied and include poor or irregular feeding, too much water or exercise directly after a feed, and worm infections.

RESPIRATORY PROBLEMS

Horses suffer from coughs and colds as much as humans and the causes can be just as varied. Some are viral infections, others bacterial problems, some allergies and others are hereditary. They can be seriously infectious and the sick horse should be isolated from its companions.

All horses should be vaccinated against influenza. It is highly infectious and can make the horse suffer for several months, so most good livery stables insist that all horses are vaccinated before they will accept them.

If a horse does contract the influenza virus it will have a high temperature, a discharge from the nostrils which thickens as the illness progresses, a persistent cough and swollen glands under the jaw. The standard treatment is antibiotics to reduce the horse's temperature and to clear up any secondary bacterial infections, and cough electuaries and linctuses to soothe the coughing.

Other viruses, however, can produce influenza-like symptoms but are only the horse equivalent of the human cold. And like the human cold there is no effective treatment, but as the infection is usually short-lived, it has no long-lasting effects. Immunity is short-lived, however, and re-infection can occur quite regularly. The best treatment is rest, so do not work the horse while it is ill.

Strangles is a bacterial infection and creates similar symptoms to influenza. As the illness progresses the swollen glands under the jaw enlarge and form abscesses which break and discharge pus through the horse's skin. Strangles can be passed on through contact with infected grooming kit and stable equipment. This is a job for the veterinarian who will administer antibiotics. The abscesses may need to be drawn with hot fomentations.

Some horses develop a persistent harsh dry cough and when they breathe out they give a double heave of the chest. This was traditionally known as broken wind, but today is called chronic obstructive pulmonary disease (COPD). The cause has been identified as lung damage due to the horse breathing in fungal spores from food and bedding carried in the air in stables. The allergic reaction to the spores causes the airways in the lungs to constrict and this reduces the airflow in the lungs as a whole.

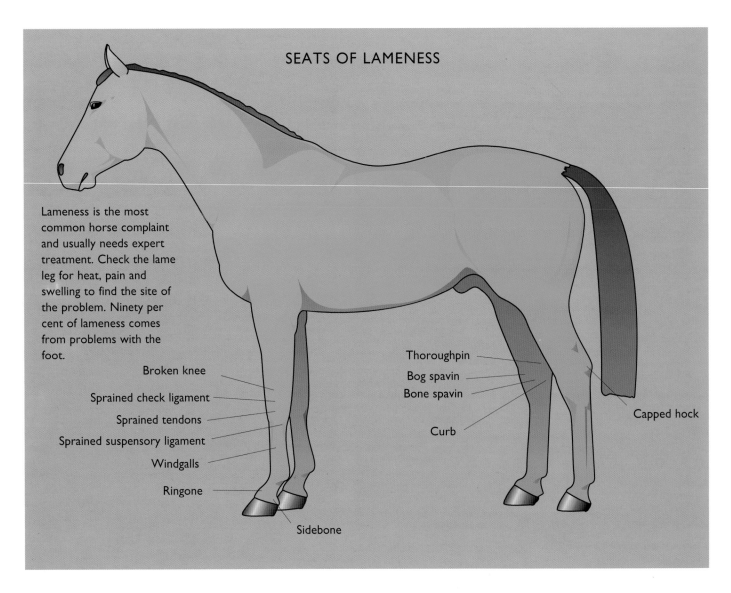

SEATS OF LAMENESS

Lameness is the most common horse complaint and usually needs expert treatment. Check the lame leg for heat, pain and swelling to find the site of the problem. Ninety per cent of lameness comes from problems with the foot.

Broken knee

Sprained check ligament

Sprained tendons

Sprained suspensory ligament

Windgalls

Ringone

Sidebone

Thoroughpin

Bog spavin

Bone spavin

Curb

Capped hock

There is no cure for this illness, although symptoms can be alleviated by treatment using drugs similar to the ones used to treat asthma in humans.

Preventative measures are the best course of action. Fresh hay and bedding contain less spores than old material and make sure you keep the horse out of the stable for at least half an hour after shaking up bedding as this will allow the spores to settle. Good ventilation in the stable is also essential. Soaking a hay-net in water for five minutes before giving it to the horse will also help.

FEET AND LEGS

The most vulnerable part of a horse are its legs and feet as the legs have to take knocks without a protective fleshy covering, carry the entire weight of the horse and can twist on rough ground if the horse stumbles. The legs take a continual pounding,

particularly on hard ground, and the feet can be damaged by poor shoeing, stray stones, sharp objects, and are highly susceptible to wet conditions, fever and inflammation. Any damage to the horse's limbs must be taken seriously and any sign of lameness examined by a veterinarian and diagnosed. Some problems are progressive and incurable if left too long.

Lameness can be checked by asking someone to lead the horse at a slow trot to see if it favours a particular leg. Look out for the way it shifts its weight. Turning the horse usually makes the symptoms more marked. If a foreleg is giving problems the horse will drop its head as the other one touches the ground. Watch if he places his weight more on one hindleg than the other. When you have identified which leg is the problem, treatment is best left to the experts – veterinarian, farrier or blacksmith.

RIGHT: *A healthy polo pony, alert and bright-eyed.*

INDEX

Page numbers in italic refer to the illustrations.

Aids, 59–60
American breeds, 24–5
Andalusian horse, *17*
Appaloosa, 22, *24*, 25
Arabian, 14, *14*, *17–19*, *19*, 27, *47*, *88*
auctions, 11

Back protectors, 36, *38*
backing, 64, 75
bad habits, 75–7
bandages, tail, 54, *55*
bedding, 50
biting, 76, *76*
bitless bridles, 32–4, *32*
bits, 30–4, *32*, 38
blankets, 39–40, *39*
boots, rider's, 36, 79, 83
boxing, 13, 76, *76*, 77
breathing, 91
breastplates, 30
breeds, 12, 18–27
bridles, *32–5*, *34–6*
bridoon, 31, *32*
British native breeds, 21–2
browbands, 34
bucking, 75
buying horses, 10–17

Canter, *54*, 64, 71, 72, 74–5
character, horse's, 12–13
chronic obstructive pulmonary disease (COPD), 93–4
cleaning tack, 37–9
clipping, 54, *55*
clothing, 36, 79, 83
clubs, 79
Clydesdale, 22, 27
coat, 14
    clipping, 54, *55*
    colours, 22
colic, 93
colours, 22
competing, 79–86
conformation, 12, 14, *15*
coughs, 93
cribbing, 12
cuts and bruises, 93

Daily routines, 70
Dales pony, 21, 22
Dartmoor pony, 21, 22
dismounting, 63
double bridles, 31–2, *32*, *35*

dressage, *59*, 84, 86, *87*
dressage saddles, 29, *29*

Ears, conformation, 14
etiquette, 83
eventing, 86, *86*
exercise, 50–1, 70–1, *70*
Exmoor pony, *20*, 21, 22
eyes:
    cleaning, *52*
    conformation, 14

Falling, *68*, 69
feeding, 43–5
feet, 13–14, *15*
    lameness, 94
    picking out, *53*
Fell pony, 21, *21*, 22
fields, 10–11, 44, 45–7, *46*
figures of eight, 71, 72, *73*
financial checklist, 10
first–aid kit, 90, *90*
fitness, 70–1
freeze marking, 47, *47*

Gag bits, 32
gaits, 64–5, *65*, 71
gallop, 65, 71
gates, 47
geldings, 12
girths, 30, *31*, 40
good manners, 74–5, 83
grass, 43–4
grooming, 37, 51–4, *52–4*, 71, 83
gymkhanas, 79–80, *81*

Hackamores, 32–4, *32*
halt, 64, 75
hats, 36, 79, 83
hay, 44
hay–nets, 43, *43*, 45
head:
    conformation, 14
    markings, *22*
head collars, 37
health, 89–94
heavy breeds, 27
hedges, 47
Highland pony, 22
hocks, conformation, 14, *15*
hooves, 14, *15*, 48–9

Icelandic pony, 27
illness, 89–94
immunization, 89, 93
influenza, 93
Irish martingales, 37

Jackets, 36, 79, 83
jodhpurs, 36, 79, 83
jumping, 16, 66–7, *66–9*, 84, *84–5*

Kicking, 77

Lameness, 92, 94, *94*
laminitis, 92
leading reins, 37
learning to ride, 9
legs, 13–14, *15*
    lameness, 94
    leg protectors, 40, *40*
    markings, *22*
lice, 92
livery, 11
lungeing, *58*, 63, 71, 72

Manes, 54
    plaiting, *82*
manners, 74–5, 83
mares, 12
markings, *22*
martingales, 36–7
Morgan, 22, 24
mounting, 62, *62*
mouth, 13
mucking out, 50, *50*
mud fever, 93

Native breeds, 21–2
neck, conformation, 14
New Forest pony, 21, 22
nosebands, 36
numnahs, 29

Pasture, 10–11, 44, 45–7, *46*
pelham bits, 31, *32*, *34*
Percheron, 22, 27
plaiting, *82*
poisonous plants, 48
pulse, 91

Quarter Horse, 22, 24, 25

Rain scald, 93
rearing, 75–6, *76–7*
reins, 36, 37, 40, 59
respiratory problems, 93–4
riders, training, 57–69
ringworm, 91
road safety, 80
rugs, 39, 47
running martingales, 36–7

Saddlebred, 22, 24, *25*
saddle covers, 36

saddles, *28–30*, *29–30*, 36, 38, 40, 57
seat, 58–9, *60–1*
security, 47
sharing horses, 11
shelters, 45
Shetland pony, *13*, 22, *23*
Shire, 22, *26*, 27
shoeing, 47–9, *48*
show-jumping, 84
showing, 79–86
skin diseases, 91–2
snaffle bits, 31, *32*, *33*
stables, 11, 49–50, *49*, *50*
Standardbred, 22, 25
stirrups, 30, 38, 57, 59
strangles, 93
Suffolk, 22, 27
sweet itch, 92

Tack, 29–40
tacking up, 36
tails, 54
    bandaging, 54, *55*
    plaiting, *82*
teeth, 91, *91*
temperature, 91, *91*
Tennessee Walking Horse, 22, 25
Thoroughbred, 19, 27
training, 57–77
treats, 48
trekking, *80*
trot, 64, *65*, 71, 74–5

Vaccination, 89, 93
veterinary inspections, 13, *14*
vices, 12

Walk, 64, *65*, *70*, 71, 74
warble flies, 92
washing down, *71*
water, drinking, 44–5
weaving, 12
Welsh Cob, 21, 22, *23*
Welsh Mountain pony, 22, *23*
Welsh pony, 22
Western tack, 40, *41*
working hunter classes, 84
worms, 47, 89–91